SIN

Satan's Playground

Kelly Bauserman

Order this book online at www.trafford.com
or email orders@trafford.com

Most Trafford titles are also available at major online book retailers.

Printed in the United States of America.

ISBN: 978-1-4269-4542-7 (sc)
ISBN: 978-1-4269-4543-4 (hc)
ISBN: 978-1-4269-4544-1 (e)

Library of Congress Control Number: 2010915290

*Our mission is to efficiently provide the world's finest, most comprehensive book publishing
service, enabling every author to experience success. To find out how to publish your book,
your way, and have it available worldwide, visit us online at www.trafford.com*

Trafford rev. 11/01/2010

 www.trafford.com

North America & international
toll-free: 1 888 232 4444 (USA & Canada)
phone: 250 383 6864 ♦ fax: 812 355 4082

Chapter 1

All creation knows its predators- except man. We are not at the top of the food chain; Satan is on this world. We need to realize who hunts us- the Devil and his demons- and do as the WORD says:

Be sober; be vigilant; because your adversary the Devil, as a roaring lion, walks about seeking whom he may devour.

(1st PETER 5:8.)

Every animal whether fish, mammal, bird or creeping thing, instinctively knows its predators, and how to use their own GOD given defenses against those predators; all instinctively; except fallen man. We as the human race are ignorant, and even indifferent to <u>our</u> predator: Satan, the Devil.

Without a doubt, we *are* human; and because Satan is here on this earth, there will be temptation to sin. Believe it or not, we are all still temptable in one way or another; for we are an unfinished work, until LORD JESUS takes us Home. Do you know why Satan wants us to sin? Because he knows sin separates us from our FATHER GOD, and drives a wedge between what we are meant to walk in and what we do walk in, as far as HIS peace and the power of the HOLY SPIRIT. Satan does not want us to be like LORD JESUS.

Sins committed by Christians who are more advanced into the sanctification process are easier to identify to the individual because as one gets closer to FATHER GOD, as Paul said, "I am the chiefest of sinners;" we recognize our own fallibility; but for anyone to say that they are sinless, is utterly futile, for there is but One Who is, and was totally sinless- that is my LORD JESUS CHRIST.

As the sanctification process proceeds in an individual, they will become less and less temptable with the obvious things; the temptations of Satan then become more subtle; pride becomes the enemy of those who are experienced in their walk with the LORD; in my own experience, I have seen it work this way; I have also seen it work another way, in my own life, which is both humiliating, and embarrassing to reveal, but I feel I am lead of the HOLY SPIRIT to divulge secrets of my life. It should make an interesting story, especially if you have read my first two books, CHOSEN VESSEL, and CHANGING VESSEL. The other way it works is that Satan will intensify his attacks; obstinately trying to make me fall anyway he knows I am still prone to falling to his temptations. This is why the HOLY SPIRIT's job of dredging up the old nature to be confessed and forgiven, and ultimately gotten rid of, is so important.

Never assume you are untemptable; because the moment you do, Satan will hit you with the demons of pride, and down you'll go. It's like handing candy to a child; Satan must enjoy feeling the pride swell in our hearts, knowing the downfall that is coming per the WORD of GOD (PROVERBS 16:18). And yes, Satan knows full well, the WORD, and how to turn it, twist it, and conform it to his own evil uses. Praise FATHER GOD, though, that HE is in control of what Satan does, and how far he will go in any of our lives; and to what extent we are tempted, for as the WORD says:

> Therefore let him who thinks he stands take heed lest he fall. No temptation has overtaken you except such as is common to man; but GOD *is* faithful, who will not allow you to be tempted beyond what you are able, but with the temptation will also make the way of escape, that you may be able to bear *it*.

(1ˢᵗCORINTHIANS 10: 12, 13.)

How many times have you been tempted with pleasurable things, and found the courage and the selflessness to seek the way out that GOD describes in this verse? I have several times; but not every time. Who wants to turn down a temptation that makes us feel good, especially in a world full of negatives and hateful things? *We* have to, that's who! Webster's Dictionary describes "tempt" as, "to entice to do wrong by promise of pleasure or gain." Webster agrees with FATHER GOD. Again, the WORD:

> Then JESUS said to HIS disciples, "If anyone desires to come after ME, let him deny himself, and take up his cross and follow ME. For whoever desires to save his life, will lose it, but whoever loses his life for MY sake will find it.
>
> (MATTHEW 16:24, 25.)

I take it that losing my own life for LORD JESUS' sake means one thing: denying myself when I am tempted. And man, am I tempted! It takes a lot of integrity to say no to some of the things that I have been tempted with, in the intensity that they have been delivered to me. I want to come right out and tell you what they are, but it isn't quite time yet.

> "Watch and pray, lest you enter into temptation. The spirit indeed *is* willing, but the flesh *is* weak."
>
> (MATTHEW 26:41.)

Notice HE said, "is WEAK," not unable. We have something that is called "choice." It's an ugly thing, if you think about it in the wrong way. But to think about it in the right way is to know that we *can* choose right when tempted with wrong. And we have the precious HOLY SPIRIT to energize and uplift us in our continuous fight against our enemy, Satan.

Some of my roughest battles I have had have been with my "self;" That is to say, the part of me that holds on to the world and its temptations manifested by Satan. What does the WORD say about the world?

Not the enormous globe we call earth, but the realm of self induced deception that holds us captive by our own choices. The WORD says,

> "For what is a man profited, if he shall gain the whole world, and lose his own soul?"

> (MATTHEW 16:26.)

This world veils our eyes from the Spiritual with materialism, and lusts which come in many various forms, such as for power, money, and fornication; driving the people of this earth to the point of losing their own souls, if unguided by the HOLY SPIRIT. This will ultimately be a battle with our own selves for control of our destinies. We, who have been chosen before the foundation of the world, know that predestination means we are protected from this veil and its deception. As LORD JESUS said in MATTHEW 24:4, "Take heed that no man deceive you." I believe this means Satan's deception through men and women aimed at us.

FATHER GOD has given us HIS WORD, and in it the blueprint for withstanding the Devil, and his demons. The WORD says:

> Finally, my brethren, be strong in the LORD and in the power of HIS might. Put on the whole armor of GOD, that you may be able to stand against the wiles of the Devil. For we do not wrestle against flesh and blood, but against principalities, against powers, against the rulers of the darkness of this age, against spiritual hosts of wickedness in high *places*. Therefore take up the whole armor of GOD, that you may be able to stand in the evil day, and having done all, to stand.

> (EPHESIANS 6:10-13.)

I will write and explain my view of the whole armor of GOD in a few moments. Right now I want to stress a point; as LORD JESUS said in 2nd CORINTHIANS 12:9, "MY grace is sufficient for thee: for MY strength is made perfect in weakness." When we are at our weakest, LORD JESUS is strong in our behalf. It seems that whenever my flesh is weak, that's when FATHER GOD allows Satan to tempt me the strongest. I believe that is to build my faith and strengthen me in my fight against the Devil and my "self," which likes to indulge in sin at my weakest points.

Satan's demons are standing by ready to take advantage of our lusts, by attempting to infiltrate our minds when they start to wander (as mine does quite frequently). I was sitting, thinking of a card game I had played the other day. One of the hands was quite humorous, and I was thinking about the way it turned out. All of a sudden, an evil thought came to my mind. I had forgotten about our enemy and let my guard down for just a moment. I shook my head violently to rid my mind of Satan's input, which worked to a degree; it was then my LORD JESUS showed me that HE allows these things to happen so I can explain the process to you and glorify HIM at the same time. It was shown to me that Satan's demons must approach me in a way consistent with the WORD; it being as follows:

Let no man say when he is tempted, I am tempted of GOD: for GOD cannot be tempted with evil, neither tempteth HE any man: but every man is tempted, when he is drawn away of his own lust, and enticed. Then when lust hath conceived, it bringeth forth sin: and sin, when it is finished, bringeth forth death.

(JAMES 1:13-15.)

I was tempted by a demon of Satan that used planted seeds that lay dormant until just now when Satan saw an opening to lure my mind in lust. It just makes it ever more clear that I need to do as the WORD says:

Stand therefore, having girded your waist with truth, having put on the breastplate of righteousness, and having shod your feet with the preparation of the gospel of peace; above all, taking the shield of faith with which you will be able to quench all the fiery darts of the wicked one. And take the helmet of salvation, and the sword of the SPIRIT, which is the WORD of GOD; praying always with all prayer and supplication in the SPIRIT, being watchful to this end with all perseverance and supplication for all the Saints-

(EPHESIANS 6:14-18.)

Now I said that I would explain the parts of the armor; it will be with my own understanding and the WORD. Let's begin with girding your waist with truth. When the LORD first had me read this in EPHESIANS, it was read with the King James Version, which substitutes "loins" for waist. That hits me harder, I think. How do I say this tactfully, LORD JESUS? It is my sexual drives that must be girded, or held in check, with truth. The truth being from the WORD, where it says:

You shall not commit adultery.

(EXODUS 20:14.)

And again,

"You have heard that it was said to those of old, 'You shall not commit adultery.' But I say to you that whoever looks at a woman to lust after her has already committed adultery with her in his heart."

(MATTHEW 5:27, 28.)

The WORD describes in 1st CORINTHIANS 6:13-20, the relationship of the body to the LORD, and our relationship to the bodies' we are in; and the dangers of fornication, or sexual immorality, as it is stated in the New King James Version:

Foods for the stomach and the stomach for foods, but GOD will destroy both it and them. Now the body *is* not for sexual immorality but for the LORD, and the LORD for the body. And GOD both raised up the LORD and will also raise us up by HIS power. Do you not know that your bodies are members of CHRIST? Shall I then take the members of CHRIST and make *them* members of a harlot? Certainly not! Or do you not know that he who is joined to a harlot is one body *with her*? For *"the two,"* HE says, *"shall become one flesh."* (GENESIS 2:24) But he who is joined to the LORD is one spirit with HIM. Flee sexual immorality (fornication). Every sin that a man does is outside the body, but he who commits sexual immorality sins against his own body. Or do you not know that your body is the temple of the HOLY SPIRIT Who is in you, who you have from GOD, and you are not your own? For you were bought at a price; therefore glorify GOD in your body and in your spirit, which are GOD's.

(1ˢᵗ CORINTHIANS 6:13-20.)

So many people are oblivious to these truths. And yet there are those who *are* aware and still chose to do "it" anyway. The drives of the bodies we are in can be quite strong, and wanting to do the "right thing" before GOD can be a question of simply turning the other cheek, so to speak; choosing to defer to the judgment of Heaven instead of denying oneself in the first place. In other words, being willing to take what FATHER GOD has in punishment for a few moments of pleasure, which will ultimately cost you.

Then there are those who don't realize the full potential of living "clean" before FATHER GOD; choosing to fear HIM, and departing from evil. I am one of them, or at least I *was*; I have since the writing of this book come clean before my LORD and FATHER, and have a Godly fear of them now. When it talks about evil ways in the WORD of GOD, sadly it uses the examples of what women do to men; the truth of the matter is that it's just as much man's fault, if not more when it comes to adultery and fornication. Consider the WORD as an example:

For the commandment *is* a lamp, and the law a light; Reproofs of instruction *are* the way of life. To keep you from the evil woman, from the flattering tongue of a seductress. Do not lust after her beauty in your heart. Nor let her allure you with her eyelids. For by means of a harlot *a man is reduced* to a crust of bread; and an adulteress will prey upon his precious life. Can a man take fire to his bosom, and his clothes not be burned? Can one walk upon hot coals, and his feet not be seared? So *is* he who goes in to his neighbor's wife; whoever touches her shall not be innocent.

(PROVERBS 6:23-29.)

This talks about a man with his neighbor's wife; what about the rendezvous in the club downtown? Single man with a single woman, both hoping to get some relief from the pent-up frustrations of the day? What does FATHER GOD say in HIS word about that? Again, gird your loins with truth, and deny yourself, to follow LORD JESUS. Our life in CHRIST is not an easy path, especially if you are virile and hot blooded, as most young adults are; but therein lay the glory for FATHER GOD and LORD JESUS- obeying the WORD and HIS commandments going against your own grain; this glorifies Them.

The next of the armor of GOD is the Breastplate of Righteousness. My concordance has 3 whole columns on righteousness alone; most of which is in the Old Testament. But *this* I do know:

But what things were gain to me, those I counted loss for CHRIST. Yea doubtless, and I count all things *but* loss for the excellency of the knowledge of CHRIST JESUS my LORD: for whom I have suffered the loss of all things, and do count them *but* dung, that I may win CHRIST, and be found in HIM, not having mine own righteousness, which is of the law, but that which is through the faith of CHRIST, the righteousness that is of GOD by faith: that I may know HIM, and the power of HIS resurrection, and the fellowship of HIS sufferings, being made conformable unto HIS death; if by any means I might attain unto the resurrection of the dead.

(PHILPPIANS 3:7-11.)

A breastplate would seem to cover and protect the front of oneself from attacks coming at you; if I were to tie this together with what I know of Satan's attacks, forcing him to come at me from the front, always directly dealing with his effronteries with the confidence that LORD JESUS gives me, I say this- never turn your back on your enemy. A breastplate of righteousness would mean to me that the Faith in CHRIST is *the* armor of choice to protect our vital organs, i.e., the part of us that would perish without HIS Righteousness.

Shodding your feet with the preparation of the Gospel of Peace, means to me being prepared at all times to speak and act upon the defense of the Gospel of our LORD JESUS; to speak boldly, as we should. The days are already here where speaking out in defense of the Gospel will not only cause animosity and open hatred, but also in some countries cause a person to be put in prison, or killed outright, all of which LORD JESUS told us would come. I envision that this country, if the progression of self indulgence, and self willed life styles persist will end up doing the same to those who stand in defense of the Gospel of LORD JESUS CHRIST. It's about time for the Antichrist to show his ugly head. Satan is preparing his followers (whether they know it or not) to stand up and shout hatred and death to the Body of CHRIST; we *must* stand strong and united; stand against the onslaught of satanic opposition to the freeing of those who are captive to him.

The shield of faith is next talked about in the WORD of GOD. The ability is given us to quench all the fiery darts of the wicked one. What fiery darts, you may ask? The answers get a little deep, and please bear with me as I follow the HOLY SPIRIT's lead on this.

Comments that tear at our faith can come from three different sources; all of which I am intimately acquainted with. First, come the darts from the wicked one himself, through our "selves." Our minds are open playgrounds for him to speak, depending on how much the LORD JESUS allows him entrance (this I say because HE uses this to teach me to resist the Devil; all a part of the sanctification process.) Satan uses phrases like, "I should have…," and, "I'm not even saved because…," or "the LORD doesn't love me…," making the individual think it is they who are speaking these things of themselves. Doubt and condemnation are the result of his voice through our "selves."

Secondly, come the comments or "fiery darts" from the people that surround us. Now, to those who can receive this, I say this: it is Satan speaking through them to attack you, either by directly speaking through their vessels, or he has manipulated them into believing lies, so they attack on their own, your position on the Gospel of LORD JESUS CHRIST. A good example of this comes from the WORD in MATTHEW 16:

> From that time forth began JESUS to show unto HIS disciples, how that HE must go unto Jerusalem, and suffer many things of the elders and the chief priests and scribes, and be killed, and be raised again the third day. Then Peter took HIM, and began to rebuke HIM, saying, be it far from THEE, LORD: this shall not be unto THEE. But HE turned and said unto Peter, "Get thee behind ME, Satan: thou art an offence unto ME: for thou savorest not the things that be of GOD, but those that be of men."
>
> (MATTHEW 16:21-23.)

LORD JESUS knew that it was Satan speaking through Peter; and lying to Peter so that he thought those words were his own. Peter thought that he was doing the right thing, in rebuking the LORD's destiny. It is the same with us; each time we open our mouths to speak, the origin of the words is either Satan, or the SPIRIT of FATHER GOD. If our words come from one of two sources, where are we in all of this? We are in the middle of these two opposing forces. Our voice is often heard in the choices we make to speak. It then makes it ever more clear what the WORD says about idle words. Webster's Dictionary describes idle words as "lacking worth;" ie, vain chatter. To put it in an Eternal perspective, our words should be of Heavenly things, or as EPHESIANS 4 says, to **edify the hearer.**

The third and most difficult to deal with are the voices of schizophrenia, for even though they come from a part of me, they still seem to be speaking from an entity that I cannot see. They tear at my faith, and speak some of the most disgusting and blasphemous things that I've ever had the dismay to hear. I pray for everyone who has the disease, for I know what it is like to not know, first of all, where these voices are coming from, but also whether to believe what's being said. It is truly maddening. I also believe schizophrenia is an attack from Satan's arsenal.

To me, putting on the helmet of salvation means to carry the knowledge of our own salvation in CHRIST JESUS, not allowing our enemy to steal our peace from our minds. It is the portion of armor that protects us from from the power and effects of sin. If Satan can't get to our minds, he's been rendered powerless; though this doesn't mean he gives up. Consider Job. Satan approached GOD to get at Job; GOD told him in JOB 1:12, "Satan, behold all that he has is in your power; only do not lay a hand on him." The story goes on to tell of how he lost all of his livestock, his children were all killed tragically, and yet Job in his grief, fell down upon the ground and worshipped GOD. In all this, Job did not sin, nor charge GOD foolishly. Oh, that we would take Job's example when we are attacked by Satan.

Next, FATHER GOD allowed Satan to attack Job's body. His wife and friends blamed him, or entreated him to blame GOD. He was surrounded by negative input, saying in chapter 19, verse 2, "How long will you vex my soul, and break me in pieces with words?" In the midst of his affliction, Job still held on to his faith and honored GOD. There is so much more to this story; if you need to be strengthened in resolve in any situation you are encountering, read about Job.

Lastly, the final piece of armor is an offensive weapon; namely the Sword of the SPIRIT, or the WORD of GOD, with which we can drive back the demons and especially Satan, himself, away from our homes, our children, and our own lives; causing him to back away from our finances; making him stay away from our minds and hearts, and from stealing our peace; preventing him from destroying our homes and the lives within. The family that reads the WORD together will more likely stay together than one where the TV is on all the time. One thing is for sure-they will have less bickering and lack of respect going towards each other. They will be a closer knit family, too.

For the WORD of GOD is living, and powerful, and sharper than any two edged sword, piercing even to the division of soul and spirit, and of joints and marrow, and is a discerner of the thoughts and intents of the heart.

(HEBREWS 4:12.)

I lean upon the WORD of GOD with all my being, knowing within myself that it is truth, despite the fiery darts from people I know saying that it was written by man. They just don't have a clue about the power of the SPIRIT of GOD being the inspiration to write, and HE writing the words of the Bible HIMSELF, through them. My LORD JESUS has spoken to me several times through HIS WORD; the most important being what HE said to me in HEBREWS 10, verse 36, in Rhema (the WORD alive). "For ye have need of patience, that, after ye have done the will of GOD, ye might receive the promise." I have from that time forth prayed for patience, and even though it has been a number of years ago, the patience I have been given has been used to create the books I have written, especially the one you are holding right now.

Finally, praying always with all prayer and supplication in the SPIRIT means just what it says: praying in the tongues of the SPIRIT (with or without the gift, it is possible to speak in the SPIRIT. All it takes is being baptized in the HOLY SPIRIT). I didn't have the prayer language until I went to our church and asked our pastor to baptize me in the HOLY SPIRIT. He laid his hands on my head and spoke to LORD JESUS, asking HIM to do just that, and then told me to speak. What came forth from my lips was a language I have come to recognize as the Precious HOLY SPIRIT's lovely and powerful voice; I spoke clearly, and strongly, and one of my brothers in our LORD JESUS said that he felt that one way back where he was! I have had it ever since. It was asked for me to be able to pray with the understanding as well, which I have received, and walk in to this day. Such is the much needed armor of GOD. Walking with each piece in place, one would be able to do as the WORD says, having done all, to stand.

I would like to share with you some of the experiences I have had that wearing the armor of GOD protected me; most have been attacks from the evil one himself, and his demons, directly. He has planted seeds of doubt in me that I am not saved, because I have sinned before my FATHER GOD, willingly. He has perverted the WORD to try and convince me that it is hopeless to continue to confess my sins, and be forgiven, again and AGAIN. These seeds my LORD has lead me to command Satan to uproot, and all effects of their presence removed from me; all in my Holy LORD JESUS' Name, and Praise GOD! He has done as he was commanded.

Next, Satan would speak to me, telling me it is futile to command him away, for he will just come right back and plant more seeds. I tell you, he is relentless in my life. I praise my LORD JESUS, and my Holy Heavenly FATHER that they are always right there, ready to fight in the SPIRIT, with my angel beside me any onslaught that Satan brings my way.

This, the helmet of salvation held my head in peace that I am saved to this day, and by FATHER GOD's Grace, and Mercy, will continue in my Holy LORD JESUS, believing and trusting in HIM till my death, or HIS glorious return for we who believe in HIM. And how can you not believe in HIM? HE is so real and personable, and loves us more than any of us will ever know on this earth.

In conjunction with the helmet of salvation, I have used the sword of the SPIRIT to counter- attack Satan when he would try to convince me that I wasn't worthy of GOD's Kingdom, telling me that I was nothing but a worthless sinner, who would never amount to anything GOD could use. The LORD spoke through my voice to Satan, and told him that HE died for me, and that I am HIS FATHER's son, and HIS Brother. Also, that I would fulfill HIS FATHER's Holy perfect will. I have been praying for that to happen ever since, and now I have a third book in the works, all three written by the power and assistance of the HOLY SPIRIT; my LORD JESUS enabling me to get the first two published, and I am sure, this one that you are holding right now.

There is an interesting story behind this book. By now you know that I have schizophrenia; and the insights that I have been given in these books come straight from the HOLY SPIRIT of GOD. I was told by the voice I consider to be my Holy LORD JESUS' that I was going to be taken Home after completing this book. I was actually told this; and it is confirmed on a daily basis. Now my psychotherapist and I have spoken at length about this, and we have come to the point of having a back-up plan if it should not happen within the time frame I believe I came up with. I even today asked FATHER GOD if I did wrong in telling my therapist a time frame, and HE spoke again, and said, "MY time is MY time alone." I am at a loss for words in this case. After completing the book you are now holding, it could be years or days after its completion that I am taken Home. Meanwhile, I look like a fool. It is a good thing I don't really care what people think about this particular manifestation of FATHER GOD's mercy.

The back-up plan consists of valued actions taken to ensure my security remains prayerfully in my LORD JESUS CHRIST in faith. In other words, I don't want to start to doubt my LORD's verbal leadings, just because I was not taken home in the time I thought I would be after completing this book. It will become common knowledge that I have passed away if it comes about after finishing "SIN;" and my passing will have repercussions from the Mental Health Unit of the V.A. to everyone who reads my books. They will all know that I indeed did hear from my Holy LORD JESUS.

If it does not happen, I am instructed to see it as an opportunity to see my schizophrenic voices as what they are-deceiving, and self diluting. I will at that time re-evaluate what I consider to be the LORD's voice. Right now, though, I am 100% confident that I am going to be taken Home. What a witness, when that does happen.

Chapter 2

I look at two different lives; mine, and that of one of my brother's in CHRIST. His life seems idyllic; he is prospering, and full of life; he has a wonderful wife, obedient, and saved children, and grandchildren; he is fulfilling FATHER GOD's Holy perfect will for his life. Mine? My children are not saved, and I believe the LORD told me a few weeks ago, that HE was going to have to take me out of the way for them to enter the Kingdom of my LORD JESUS CHRIST. Life just seems so difficult for me; the difference? Sin. I readily admit to this.

The desire to perform the Holy perfect will of my FATHER GOD is there; my spirit is willing, and my flesh is under submission; at least for the most part. Self control-one of the fruits of the HOLY SPIRIT, is being deployed on my flesh. I *am* on the right path to sanctification. What am I complaining about? I am complaining that I have a harder time getting the same results that my brother in CHRIST JESUS is getting, with half the effort. Let me explain.

Tithing 10% of what comes in; I had been doing just that. Things got tight, and I faltered, giving only a portion of the 10% to FATHER GOD. He has honored that portion; keeping my head above water; I was able through prayer to finance a merchandising package with my publisher without going under, praise GOD. Now that is under the bridge, I will be able to build again my finances, and begin again to tithe like I was. Looking at it in the secular way, it's crazy to give 10% of what is brought in to a Christian organization. But I'm not looking at it in a secular way. I know that tithing is a way of bringing about a prospering of our finances, and also, as the WORD says in MALACHI chapter 3, preventing the devourer from getting to our lives:

> Bring all the tithes into the storehouse, that there may be food in MY house. And try ME in this, says the LORD of hosts, "If I will not open for you the windows of Heaven and pour out for you *such* blessing that *there will not be room* enough *to receive it.* And I will rebuke the devourer for your sakes, so that he will not destroy the fruit of your ground, nor shall the vine fail to bear fruit for you in the field," says the LORD of hosts.
>
> (MALACHI 3:10,11.)

I mean this really blesses the LORD, when we tithe. As the WORD says again:

> Honor the LORD with your possessions and with the first fruits of all your increase; so your barns will be filled with plenty, and your vats will overflow with new wine.
>
> (PROVERBS 3:9,10.)

Am I saying that not tithing is a sin? Yes, I am; for the WORD says again:

> Will a man rob GOD? Yet you have robbed ME. But you say, wherein have we robbed YOU? In tithes and offerings.
>
> (MALACHI 3:8.)

Thou shalt not steal, it says. I have robbed FATHER GOD and used HIS money for my own purposes. All HE asks is just 10% off the original income. Don't get me wrong, I *am* blessed. But how much more would I, will I, when I am tithing again as I should? Tremendously, I am guessing.

I received good counsel at church the other Sunday. The person I spoke with advised me to command Satan off of my children's lives. For him to uncover their eyes, that they might see; and to uncover their ears that they might hear what the HOLY SPIRIT is saying to them; also to bind Satan off of their lives, enabling the HOLY SPIRIT to continue to work in their lives. I am going to do this from this moment on, till they are safely in the fold. The truth that I will be taken out of the way for them to enter the Kingdom means that I will continue till the day I am taken Home to pray for their salvation in LORD JESUS, and to continue to praise FATHER GOD and LORD JESUS for saving them.

There again the accountability of my own life, and it's sins that I have, and do commit at times, speak against doing this; for it makes sense that I would need to be right with the LORD JESUS for Satan to break off his attack on my children. But then Satan must respond to what he is commanded in LORD JESUS' Name, regardless of my spiritual condition; or am I wrong? I repent of the things that I have been doing, thinking, and desiring. I repent directly to you, my Holy Heavenly FATHER, in Your Name, my Holy LORD JESUS. I pray each morning for a constant state of repentance in this vessel, and for down to the ground humility continually in this vessel. Now that is accomplished, I should be in the clear to bind Satan off of my children. And when the tithes are flowing back out to their respective places, the LORD will rebuke the devourer for me in my life, and in my children's lives, and my flock's lives. I believe it! Once set in motion, these things will continue even after my passing from life to life eternal.

Chapter 3

The lies of Satan; how do we, as the Body of CHRIST, dispel those lies to see our brothers and sisters into the Kingdom? I was given by my LORD JESUS insight into one of those lies, through some of the music that I listen to. Consider this: to those who as yet are unsaved, but knowledgeable of the presence and person of Satan, he has lied to them, telling them that if they turn their back on him (Satan) they will be alright. But what is the condition of "alright?"

For As the WORD says,1

For all have sinned, and fall short of the glory of GOD.

(ROMANS 3:23.)

We have all sinned, for we are born under the curse of Adam and Eve's original sin, and in need of redemption in LORD JESUS CHRIST. So what am I saying about this lie of Satan? Just turning away from Satan is not enough. We need true repentance, and must be Born Again, asking LORD JESUS into our hearts, forcing Satan out of our lives and living unto LORD JESUS.

The WORD says that Satan comes, "to steal, kill, and destroy…" (JOHN 10:10) I have seen firsthand Satan's stealing and destroying power. When the HOLY SPIRIT gave me this insight into this lie of Satan, I was driving; as I maneuvered the car into a gas station to write it down, the time it took to do this, Satan had already stolen most of what was given to me. The LORD JESUS then led me to command Satan in HIS Name, to re-establish what was given to me in full; then my LORD JESUS allowed me to realize what had just happened, how and when Satan did his stealing, and what allowed him to steal (my lack of understanding).

It's a little unnerving to realize how knowledgeable Satan is to our thoughts. Believe me, I know he is hitting me with an onslaught of sins to tempt me away from my LORD and FATHER, but then again, I know that what I am hit with is guided and watched over by FATHER GOD, ensuring that I get just enough for LORD JESUS to teach me what I need at that particular time, and that I am not overwhelmed by them.

After Satan had re-established the vision I had of his lie, I wrote it down just as I have written it out to you. Let me ask you, have you ever had a revelation given by the HOLY SPIRIT, then sometime there after you found yourself missing parts of it, or missing it altogether? I know this sounds crazy, for if Satan stole it from you, you wouldn't have anything to remember, unless LORD JESUS allowed some residue of the vision to remain, in order to teach you of Satan's ability to steal, as HE did with me just then.

During the same ride in the car, another vision of a lie of Satan came to me during another song I was listening to. To the unsaved, not being afraid of dying is a lie of Satan. If they knew of the consequences of sin in their lives, and the horror of Hell and the Lake of Fire, they would be desperately afraid, and begging everyone they know what to do about it. I hear it in the music my boys listen to. Crying out for someone to save them, not realizing that LORD JESUS is but a sincere cry away, waiting to take them gently into HIS arms.

That is another lie of Satan; that before we come to LORD JESUS, we must do all the changing of our bad habits, and ridding ourselves of the sins that we are in. Let the HOLY SPIRIT have HIS way in your life, and all these things will be taken care of in FATHER GOD's perfect timing and in HIS most gentle and non- frustrating ways. FATHER GOD *loves* you. LORD JESUS and HIS HOLY SPIRIT *love* you.

One horrifying sight I drove by on the interstate showed me Satan's power to destroy. I beheld a deep black gouge; it must have been 30 feet long out of the cement median to my left. It was shown me that Satan had plainly swiped his hand and wiped out a vehicle, probably by a semi. The burn marks were evident, where the vehicle had caught fire. All these things were shown me in the time it took to drive by the accident site.

Let me give you an example of seed planting by our enemy. It is an effrontery that sometimes gets annoying because I have to rebuke the seed planter, be it Satan, or his demons, *and* command him that the seeds planted at any particular time be uprooted and taken out of me permanently. I was driving down the bypass when I came by a car with the back tire gone. It was sitting on a jack; obviously the owner had a flat tire. As I was passing the car, the thought came to me, wouldn't it be funny to stop and push the car off the jack, leaving the car disabled, and the driver, furious. From long association with the enemy's ways, I knew where this comment came from. But the trouble with this kind of seed planting is not so obvious. Left undealt with, it could very well manifest itself in deviant behavior. I have a bad tendency to forget what happens to me; the truth is that much of it is stolen from me by Satan. He would of course want me to forget his seed planting on this day, so he could manifest those seeds into plants or trees of unrighteous behavior. Praise be to my Holy LORD JESUS, that HE doesn't let me forget the important things that I need to write about. I commanded Satan to stop his comments, and take his seeds that he planted and remove them permanently from me; all in my LORD JESUS' Name. I immediately felt the impression leave me, and I believe that all the seeds are gone as well, in faith. Praise FATHER GOD!

During the preceding night, I was given direction for what to write here now. It is called "regrets;" The "should haves," the "could haves," and the "would haves," that bother us in the middle of the night, and leave us wanting to do something that's probably not in the best interests of ourselves. Let me give you an example.

Sin committed in the name of regret is one of the hardest to be repentant for. I for one dealt with this following regret for *years* before the LORD JESUS took it away from me. It still sometimes leaves me wide awake thinking in the middle of the night.

A lady friend of mine from *way back*, was on my "hit list" of hot prospects to sleep with. But, being a virgin, and not acquainted with the ways of girls in general, I lost out on many good opportunities; then came the night of the party. We were gathered together for one last good drunk before we all moved on.

Being as naïve as I was back then, "painfully naïve," as I recall it now; I was oblivious to the come- ons of more than one girl in my circle of "prospects." The lady friend I was speaking about was at the party that night. Knowing that I was going to be at the party, was waiting for the opportune time to get me alone. To make a short story even shorter, I was oblivious to the meal that was being served to me on a silver platter; upon reflection, I couldn't have had it any better. I just didn't know what I had at the time. Beat *that* for regrets!

Actually, I can beat it; read on: back when I lived in Iowa, I must have been about 10 years of age; going to Knox Presbyterian Church with my mom. One Sunday we were sitting in our pew, listening to the sermon, when the HOLY GHOST came upon me so strong, that I just sobbed, not knowing what was happening to me. LORD JESUS was calling me to come to HIM, and ask HIM into my heart. My sweet mother didn't lead me to repentance, but just left me to sob until the feeling passed; *without* asking LORD JESUS into my heart. Do you *know* the things I could and would have been spared if I had only asked HIM into my heart at that young age? I can only imagine where I'd be and what I would be accomplishing for HIS Kingdom by now. Now *that* is a large regret; one that I try not to think about too often. I have talked it over what I would have accomplished with my FATHER GOD and my LORD JESUS. They just want me to praise them for what is right now, and the praise is this: that even though things could have been a lot different, FATHER GOD still had a plan for the rest of my life; including the book that you are now holding.

If maybe something in these words inspires someone to deal with their regrets, I will have accomplished what I set out to do with these tales of my exploits.

Another time I was led to witness to one of my friends who was asking about JESUS, and what he needed in regards to HIM. I totally blew that opportunity, by listening to the majority of the fellows that were sitting there in the room with us. I can only pray for this friend that FATHER GOD leads him to LORD JESUS again, and that he accepts HIM into his heart. I think about this from time to time, and it helps me to take advantage of situations where I *know* that GOD is leading me to witness. The one thing I don't want to do is beat myself up for things that I failed to do, knowing that they are forgiven by my LORD JESUS, and in this case, that HE *will* have mercy upon my friend to see him into the Kingdom.

Another thing I don't want to do is stand before the Throne, and explain why I didn't do what FATHER GOD was obviously leading me to do for HIS SON, and HIS Kingdom; and for my brothers and sisters who as it stands right now, are not yet in the Fold. Mercy, for me, my Holy Heavenly FATHER, that I would be right where YOU want me to be, saying and doing the things YOU want me to be doing and saying.

We *all* have regrets. What matters right now is what you do with them. Don't make a situation worse by sinning because of something you regret taking advantage of that Satan has tempted you with. I have done this for far too long now. He's like an old buddy of mine that feeds me with self indulging sins; at least he appears to be a buddy of mine. And yet he laughs with glee every time I am wounded by these acts of sin. FATHER GOD had me to confess my regrets one evening, (it took most of the evening), and we prayed for the appropriate things to take place because of the things I had failed (or rather chose) to do, or not do; I felt as though a huge weight had been lifted off my shoulders when we were done. Talk to FATHER GOD as if you were talking to a friend that you feel safe sharing your inner most feelings with; because HE *does*; and HE will never condemn you for anything you speak to HIM. Just be humble and thankful that HE does listen, and HE will remove your regrets.

Now don't be like me and try pulling yourself off of the cross once you've been crucified with CHRIST. In other words, I tried to take back the regrets once they had been taken away. Either because I felt regret (!) at the regrets being taken away, which sounds crazy, I know; or that I felt a loss of security in my "self" that my regrets had established themselves as. Take for example my first spoken of regret about my female friend: this regret fueled my desire to not miss any opportunity to sin in fornication with women. It's no wonder FATHER GOD wanted this regret to be taken away. Regrets can make us do things that are not the responsible, or the appropriate things to do. Take the following:

Back when I worked for a major department store, I met a young lady who was (is) very attractive. We started talking over the counter stuff, and I soon found out that she was a dancer at a local strip joint. I had never been to one before, and since I was so strongly attracted to this young lady, I decided to go and watch her dance. It was to become an infatuation of pure lust that I did not want to be rid of.

One of the following days at work she came by to talk to me, and I got up the courage to ask her if she would pose for me so I could draw her. Wrong? You bet it is. Did it ever come to be? No. FATHER GOD knew what kind of situation I had gotten myself into, and also knew what kind of trouble it would cause; so HE prevented HIS Child from wrecking his life, and possibly the young lady's as well.

Do I still have regrets about not doing it? Yes. It's one of the few that still remain inside of me. All this was from the regret that I had not taken advantage of the young lady at the party so long ago. Undealt with regrets can fester and manifest themselves years after the initial encounter. I still sometimes lie awake at night and think about what could have happened. The "could haves" in this scenario would have been very pleasurable, but VERY costly, and I might have never fully recovered from it had it been allowed. Satan boldly threw everything he had at me, but a merciful FATHER had HIS hand upon me even though I walked away for a little while.

All of it has been confessed several times and forgiven several times. I now no longer seek for her company. I praise FATHER

GOD that I am able to voice these things, and come to terms with feelings that few men care to talk about (but most deal with); I have gotten over this, and denied myself; picking up my cross and following my LORD JESUS again. So be it, in my LORD JESUS' Holy Name.

Chapter 4

If you are in a position of knowing that you are doing the Holy perfect will of FATHER GOD, you are blessed indeed. By continually praying in the SPIRIT, and being told that you are doing HIS will, by continuing to believe in HIS SON, take it to the next level and pray daily that your day would be one of being in the perfect place at the perfect time with apples of gold in pictures of silver; or in layman's terms, saying the perfect thing by following the SPIRIT's leading. Don't let Satan steal this motivation or allow him to destroy what FATHER GOD wants to do through you. And above all in this scenario, don't let your "self" and it's selfish ways have their way. The next verse tells of what to expect when you are "put on the spot," so to speak. I have waited upon the LORD for what to speak on numerous occasions. HIS SPIRIT has never let me down.

> "But when they deliver you up, do not worry how or what you should speak. For it will be given to you in that hour what you should speak; for it is not you who speak, but the SPIRIT of your FATHER who speaks in you."
>
> (MATTHEW 10:19,20.)

All of us should be this bold to first of all have the faith to believe we will be given what we should speak, and then when it does come directly from the SPIRIT of GOD, open our mouths with confidence that it will be the perfect thing to say at that moment.

Pray with me now. FATHER GOD, in Your Name, my LORD JESUS, please have Mercy upon me; that I would be rid of all the regrets that I have been carrying all this time. I confess that I have been unaware of their detrimental effect on my life, and I praise YOU, that YOU have given me understanding of this. Take now each of these regrets and remove them, with the regret that they *are* being taken away. I praise YOU for this, in Your Name, my LORD JESUS.

This is a first step in completing the Holy perfect will of FATHER GOD; getting rid of anything that keeps you tied to the world, and it's sins. Getting rid of regrets, even those that were to be of good things, like becoming a Child of GOD early in life, is a good thing, for regretting does nothing except keep you bound up in chains that Satan wants you to be in. Be rid of them, in my LORD JESUS' Holy Name! Praise be to YOU, my Holy Heavenly FATHER, in YOUR Name, my LORD JESUS!

I feel led to speak something about a sore subject-hypocrisy. I will not say that you must not do this or that, as far as sin goes; for I am just as guilty as the next person. As the WORD says:

You, therefore, who teach another, do you not teach yourself? You who preach that a man should not steal, do you steal? You who say, "Do not commit adultery," do you commit adultery? You who abhor idols, do you rob temples? You who make your boast in the law, do you dishonor GOD through breaking the law?

(ROMANS 2:21-23.)

I know we are not under the law, but under Grace; but it still rings true, that we who tell others the way to go, should know the way ourselves, and walk in it as well as talking it. This I have to confess now, by the leading of the HOLY SPIRIT, that I am not worthy to tell anyone the way to go, for pornography has had its ugly grasp on me since I was about 12 years of age, and still sometimes rears its powerful head to engulf me in its fumes of death. And looking at women in an adulterous fashion? Yes, I still do. I admit to these things here and now. I pray now, in Your Name, my LORD JESUS. My Holy Heavenly FATHER, I beg Your Mercy upon me right now, and ask for Your Grace, which *is* sufficient for me, to forgive me. I don't even know if telling all these people the things Your SPIRIT led me to tell just now was a good thing; I believe it was, for it lets them know the truth about me and possibly their own struggles; and maybe somewhere, somehow, they will be willing to forgive me as well, just as the You will forgive them upon their repentance. I ask that You would be willing to spend a little extra time on me, to rid me of these things. You have just now showed me that You are Omnipresent, meaning that You have all Your attention on me as well as on each of Your Children at all times. That is very comforting, Holy FATHER, and I praise You for it. I lean heavily upon You, and Your WORD, my Holy LORD JESUS, and praise You *for* You in my life. May this glorify You, and Your Name, now and forevermore. In Your Name I pray these things of You, my Holy Heavenly FATHER, and praise You for them, in Your SPIRIT, in Your Mercy, in Your Name, my Holy LORD JESUS.

Confess our faults one to another, and not judge each other for if we would all be willing to what was being told, the Body of CHRIST would be in a far better place, for we would be dealt with according to the WORD:

Confess *your* trespasses to one another, and pray for one another, that you may be healed. The effectual fervent prayer of a righteous man avails much.

(JAMES 5:16.)

Brethren, if any of you do err from the truth, and one convert him; let him know that he which converts the sinner from the error of his way shall save a soul from death, and shall hide a multitude of sins.

(JAMES 5:19,20.)

Now I don't take what people say very seriously, unless I know it is my LORD speaking through them to me; the path I have taken today in confessing these things to you, was given by my LORD and Savior, JESUS CHRIST. I trust that you won't put down this book in disgust after hearing what I have had to say in this chapter. Please read on.

I have been guilty of the sin of hypocrisy for a number of years; and it has kept me from witnessing to a number of people that I pray here and now for, that LORD JESUS would lead them into the Kingdom from someone who isn't faced with the dangerousness of hypocrisy. I wouldn't even make it known that I have been a Child of GOD for more than half of my life, until FATHER GOD had me to write my first book; and the condemnation I received from Satan was TREMENDOUS; how could anyone who does the things you do, confess to be a Child of GOD? This is what he would impart to me through my "self." Satan *is* a liar; and nothing of what he said was true. I *can*, and must confess that JESUS CHRIST is LORD of my life, and that HE is changing these awful patterns of sinning in me. I *want* people to know that the darkness hides *nothing*. What is done in the darkness *will* come to the light, and be manifest. If I choose to confess these things here and now, that *is* my choice.

Either confess them now, or wait till you are standing before the Throne; I would much rather get them out into the open now, where they can be forgiven and washed from me in my LORD JESUS' blood. I had the opportunity to tell one of my friends about this book you are holding in your hands right now. She asked me what it was about, and I answered, "sin." She got a look on her face like "Oh no, not another one." She went on to tell me, "Well, everyone sins," I agreed, but went on to say to her, that what we did with those sins is what makes the difference. I thanked my LORD JESUS for this first opportunity; for it is difficult for me to know how to describe my books. Getting these things out in the open is refreshing to me.

I will be a little more patient with the next person LORD JESUS sends my way, a little more humble as I have been humbled here today. FATHER GOD has no Mercy upon sin, only on sinners, who repent. It is FATHER GOD's goodness which leads us to repentance (ROMANS 2:4) and by that goodness, I have come to what has been asked for me, which is for repentance of my sins. Now I do care what people think; probably too much for my own good; but I will now dance for joy before my LORD and FATHER for their Mercy and their Grace upon me. You should see the smile on my face as I think of this. You should be breathing a heartfelt sigh of relief as I have just done over what has just happened. And maybe, just maybe, you have come to the same conclusion over the sins in your life. If you have, praise GOD!

Chapter 5

What do you think of the sin of pride? I grew up hearing phrases like, Stand tall, be proud; be proud of yourself, for doing everything from going to the bathroom for the first time by yourself, to the accomplishments you have done. Is there a difference between being proud of yourself, and taking pride in oneself? The latter would be of things like personal hygiene, and grooming, I would think. Where does the sin of pride come in then? Most people I have talked to think it is one of thinking that I am better than you; but pride can be to the lowliest people, if they have had challenges in their lives that wreck havoc with their sense of security. Pride is a way of shoring up the banks of their internal security.

Pride goes before destruction and a haughty spirit before a fall.

(PROVERBS 16:18.)

I believe that the LORD JESUS allows pride to enter for the destruction of the flesh, as Paul said in the WORD:

In the Name of our LORD JESUS CHRIST, when you are gathered together, along with my spirit, with the power of our LORD JESUS CHRIST, deliver such a one to Satan for the destruction of the flesh, that his spirit may be saved in the day of the LORD JESUS.

(1st CORINTHIANS 5:4,5.)

The demons of pride afflict those who are susceptible to it. If the reading of this finds your pride level anywhere but zero, heed the WORD:

The fear of the LORD is the instruction of wisdom, and before honor *is* humility.

(PROVERBS 15:33.)

And:

By humility *and* the fear of the LORD *are* riches, honor and life.

(PROVERBS 22:4.)

So we have established that it is good to have humility, and it is a prospering, life filled addition to one's life; but how does one get humility? That is if one is not already born with it. Can it be taught? The answer is yes. This goes back to family values, and the raising of our children in the fear and admonishing of the LORD JESUS CHRIST.

The problem lies here, though. A person lives his or her life being fed by Satan up until the moment that FATHER GOD leads them to LORD JESUS, and they ask HIM into their lives. You can bet that Satan will do the best job he can at compiling in you whatever will prevent you from fulfilling FATHER GOD's Holy perfect will in your life. In my own life, Satan had prepped me with a deep rooted narcissism, which ended up in a bout with attempted suicide, then the affliction of schizophrenia, which *would* have prevented me from writing these books, if the LORD JESUS hadn't had exceeding abundant mercy upon me. HIS HOLY SPIRIT has made a way for me to complete FATHER GOD's Holy perfect will in my life by leading me to ask for the patience I needed to do HIS will. Then, after I become a Child of GOD, the HOLY SPIRIT had the task of dredging up the old nature, leading me to confess what was brought to the surface, being then forgiven. That is when the daily battle for my life began.

Train up a child in the way he should go, and when he is old he will not depart from it.

(PROVERBS 22:6.)

This works both ways, you must understand. For example, if your family trained you to disrespect authority all of your impressionable years, you will probably disrespect authority when you are older as well; now some people overcome the adversities of a troubled childhood, and see growth into the righteous path. A child reared on the WORD of GOD I believe will not turn from the WORD when they are older, even though they will go through the "troubled" teen years.

Pride in our children I think is a good kind of pride; I know I want to make my Heavenly FATHER proud of me, and I am HIS Child. I want to make my Brother, LORD JESUS proud of me. So why should pride in our own children be wrong? The only thing I can see is if that pride causes pride to swell in our children's hearts towards themselves, causing them to see themselves above what they should, or see themselves above others, there would be a sin committed, and a path that would have to be expunged by the HOLY SPIRIT.

Let nothing *be done* through selfish ambition or conceit, but in lowliness of mind let each esteem others better than himself.

(PHILIPPIANS 2:3.)

Notice that it said 'esteem others better *than-*'not better *off* than himself; better off than would lead to bitterness and resentment, or outright hatred. This attitude takes a conscious effort on our part, even after you have asked LORD JESUS for the humility *to* esteem others better than yourself.

If Satan can get you to laugh at his sick and perverted jokes on TV, and laugh at the expense of others, he has hit you with pride again in yourself. I would that all TV shows that poke fun or are outright blasphemous in nature would be outlawed, but then again, the people who are in charge of creating those TV shows are probably deceived into thinking it is funny, when it is in truth Satan who is manipulating our societies through the media, moving them ever so slowly towards the mark (666), and the imminent return of my LORD JESUS CHRIST.

Isn't it incredible that someone so powerful in this earth, can remain un-noticed, and unchallenged; those who would try to change TV, end up dealing with the effects of that power, instead of dealing with its source-the Devil. At best, at family level, we can only deal with what comes out of the TV; the changes that come about in us from what we ingest. Pride in ourselves is only part of the problem. I see the main focus being on people, and what they can get from life through relationships, work, and self indulgence; mostly at the expense of other people. It says in the End Times there will come a great falling away (2ⁿᵈ THESSALONIANS 2:3,4). I believe we are on the verge of that right now. Unsaved people by the millions are filled with pride, the kind of pride that says, "I'm first, you're last, and what's in the middle doesn't count." Satan is stepping up his deception, and if we are not careful, we as the Body of CHRIST, HIS very elect, will be sucked into this attitude of complacency, and fall to this same kind of pride, only one that says, "I'm right, you're wrong and you're going to burn." Pride of this kind can only lead to a falling away, because there is no love in that type of communication. I have been guilty of this kind of pride, and it has definitely damaged relationships in my own life. Without love, the WORD says:

> And though I have *the gift of* prophecy, and understand all mysteries and all knowledge, and though I have all faith, so that I could remove mountains, but have not love, I am nothing.

> (1ˢᵗ CORINTHIANS 13:2.)

Speaking of the End Times, of which I believe that LORD JESUS' return, *is* at the doorstep; hypocrisy is definitely rampant, and because sin abounds, the love of many is waxing cold. I am speaking in the present, while the WORD speaks from 2000 years ago. This about sin and the love of many is from MATTHEW 24:12.

My point is this: Be prepared. Don't let pride get a foothold on you. Deal with the Devil, by putting him in his place (away from you and your family, and your flock). Do as the WORD says:

> Let us hear the conclusion of the whole matter: Fear GOD and keep HIS commandments, for this is the whole duty of man. For GOD will bring every work into judgment, including every secret thing, whether good or evil.

> (ECCLESIASTES 12:13,14.)

> "For the SON of Man will come in the glory of HIS FATHER with HIS angels, and then HE will reward each according to his works."

> (MATTHEW 16:27.)

Command Satan in LORD JESUS' Name! It works; and though he comes right back at me, sometimes minutes, or even seconds later, all I had to learn was to command him for the rest of the day, or on through the night, if he was trying to keep me up with thoughts that weren't my own. LORD JESUS gives us power over the enemy; the only problem is our own flesh, which is at odds with the SPIRIT; the WORD says:

> For the flesh lusteth against the SPIRIT, and the SPIRIT against the flesh: and these are contrary the one to the other: so that ye cannot do the things that ye would.

> (GALATIANS 5:17.)

So even though I wanted to resist the Devil, my flesh would get in the way, convincing me to walk away from FATHER GOD in voluntary sin. Praise my LORD JESUS that they have been working me away from the sins of my past that have kept me bound; through repentance and an abundant dose of mercy, and blessed forgiveness I am coming out from under Satan's thumb.

Chapter 6

Let's read the WORD:

"And behold, I come quickly; and MY reward *is* with ME, to give every man according as his work shall be. I am ALPHA and OMEGA, the beginning and the end, the first and the last. Blessed *are* they that do HIS commandments, that they may have the right to the tree of life, and may enter in through the gates into the city. For without *are* dogs, and sorcerers, and whoremongers, and murderers, and idolaters, and whosoever loveth and maketh a lie.

(REVELATION 22:12-15.)

And, speaking of the City, the New Jerusalem:

And there shall in no wise enter into it any thing that defileth, neither *whatsoever* worketh abomination, or *maketh* a lie: but they which are written in the LAMB's Book of Life.

(REVELATION 21:27.)

He that overcometh shall inherit all things; and I will be his GOD, and he shall be My son. But the fearful, and unbelieving, and the abominable, and murderers, and whoremongers, and sorcerers, and idolaters, and all liars, shall have their part in the lake which burneth with fire and brimstone: which is the second death.

(REVELATION 21:7,8.)

It is a sin to lie; I want to make that very clear. It has just come to me, to write a serious note about something that has been in my memory for a long time. It never even occurred to me that this was a lie until the HOLY SPIRIT showed me it was. Do you remember the episode of Star Trek where Captain Pike is in the menagerie, and the Talosians send him to the Lake of Fire? When he is brought back to the cage, they tell him that deeper in his mind are worse things. *This is a lie.* The Lake of Fire is *the* final destination, Eternal destination for those who lie. There is nothing worse. It was a seemingly harmless bit of seed planting on Satan's part, but an awful bit of lying that those who watched the show probably didn't catch. Left undealt with, this lie that only Trekkors are familiar with, could have planted seeds in our minds telling us that Hell, and the Lake of Fire are not that bad; when in truth they are to be avoided at *all costs*. And praise FATHER GOD that HE has provided *the* way, namely HIS SON, my LORD JESUS CHRIST, that those who believe in HIM should not perish, but have everlasting life (JOHN 3:16).

Let's talk about lies. We know that Satan is a liar, and the father of them (JOHN 8:44). This means that Satan and his demons will be tormented night and day Eternally for their lies, and deceit, their killing, and their stealing and destroying of our lives (I speak of the entire human race). It also stands to reason, that there were no lies in existence until Lucifer was found with iniquity in him. HE wanted to exalt his throne above that of the Most High. This was probably the first act of deception, for it is being deceived to think that you could ever exalt your throne above GOD's. After being cast down to earth, the then called Satan wanted to take down everyone that he could, to share in his punishment, starting with Adam and Eve, deceiving them into sinning, causing each of us since then to be born under their original sin.

This next part is very hard to digest. If you have strong views about abortion, please read with an open mind, and please read *all of it*. For I have come to the conclusion that this subject and the discussion of it can separate people who have strong views. My beliefs come into question, and I hope that I don't offend anyone by them.

This is another possible lie of Satan-that we have to choose to follow him; another words, that we, from birth are in a neutral state, neither GOD's nor Satan's, and that we have to choose either one; Read the WORD:

"Why do you not understand MY speech? Because you are not able to listen to MY word. You are of *your* father the Devil, and the desires of your father you want to do. He was a murderer from the beginning, and does not stand in the truth, because there is no truth in him. When he speaks a lie, he speaks from his own *resources*, for he is a liar, and the father of it."

(JOHN 8:43,44.)

LORD JESUS spoke this to bring home the point that the Jews HE was talking to had Satan as their father. I had started to write, because of this verse, it was the truth that all are Satan's children from birth, headed for the Lake of Fire, until they are lead by FATHER GOD to accept LORD JESUS into their hearts. I received counsel from a dear friend of mine that started to make me think about it. What about all the children that are aborted each and every year? Thousands upon thousands of innocent babies; are they doomed to the Lake of Fire? What about the children born with acute mental diseases, incapable of comprehending the need for salvation? Are they headed for destruction at the hand of a GOD that professes love for all mankind? Forgive me; I got a little carried away. Of course FATHER GOD loves each and every one of them. But truth is truth; without LORD JESUS, they are headed for Hell, then the Lake of Fire. Why do you think Satan wanted those people to abort those children? They had *no chance*; no say in their futures. Satan knows this. And he will take down the parents of those children too, with guilt, and condemnation up to the point that FATHER GOD intervenes.

Why do you think it is such a heavy subject? It is an *Eternal* subject. Once done, there is no turning back for those children. The best that can be done at that point is to beg forgiveness for taking a life; and after one is forgiven, forgiving themselves, and commanding Satan *away* permanently from ever mentioning it again to you in LORD JESUS' Name. That is for those that are Children of GOD that have done this thing. If you do not have LORD JESUS in your heart, you will carry the weight of the memory of this each and every time Satan reminds you of it; and he *will* remind of you of it often; and with the memory, condemning remarks that seem like they are your own. How do you think suicides happen? Satan convinces the person that the voice they are hearing is their own, telling them to take their own life; when all the while it is Satan that is talking to them through their "self." That's the way it almost happened to me.

I have been told that I take the Bible too literally. Read what LORD JESUS said about children:

Then were there brought unto HIM little children that HE should put *HIS* hands on them, and pray: and the disciples rebuked them. But JESUS said, "Suffer little children, and forbid them not, to come unto ME: for of such is the Kingdom of Heaven."

(MATTHEW 19:13,14.)

LORD JESUS also said:

"Verily I say unto you, whosoever shall not receive the Kingdom of GOD as a little child shall in no wise enter therein."

(LUKE 18:17.)

I believe there is the faith of a little child that is needed to enter the Kingdom; but of the age that a child needs to become a Child of GOD? Read again the WORD:

At the same time came the disciples unto JESUS, saying, who is the greatest in the Kingdom of Heaven? And JESUS called a little child unto HIM, and set him in the midst of them. And said, "Verily I say unto you, except ye be converted, and become as little children, ye shall not enter into the Kingdom of Heaven. Whosoever therefore shall humble himself as this little child, the same is greatest in the Kingdom of Heaven."

(MATTHEW 18:1-4.)

At what age does a child become in need of repentance? I witnessed a child of perhaps 7 years of age come to our pastor and tell him that he wanted to accept LORD JESUS into his heart. When he had done this, the child went his way back to his parents in the congregation. But listen to the WORD:

"Likewise, I say unto you, there is joy in the presence of the angels of GOD over one sinner that repenteth."

(LUKE 15:10.)

There was joy in Heaven the night that child received CHRIST into his heart. I saw this, and wanted to say something to our pastor to say to the congregation; so we as well could rejoice with the angels of Heaven at the repentance of this little one. I didn't do as FATHER GOD wanted at that appropriate moment, and the moment was lost; but the point is well taken.

Where do I go with this, I asked LORD JESUS. He spoke and said, "Where do you want it to go?" I want to get the point across that we are *all* in need of repentance. The fact that children die every day at the hands of people who know not the consequences of taking a life; for as it says in the WORD, it is an *abomination* to the LORD for hands that shed innocent blood (PROVERBS 6:17). But what I have not had to deal with is the choices of taking an innocent life; nor have I been placed in the position of feeling the need to. So I really don't have an objective viewpoint. All I know is the WORD, and what I am shown by the SPIRIT of FATHER GOD. The WORD says:

"Even so, it is not the will of your FATHER which is in Heaven, that one of these little ones should perish."

(MATTHEW 18:14.)

But they do; at least they do in the physical realm. Why then does LORD JESUS instruct us to pray that FATHER GOD's will be done in earth, as it is in Heaven, if it were being already being done? Why would it be necessary for GOD's own SON to come to this earth and *die* to save us from our sins if a person, no matter what their age, could still get into Heaven without believing in HIM? Why did this little 7 year old see the need for repentance? Why do we, as the Body of CHRIST, have to deny ourselves and follow LORD JESUS every day of our lives? Because the WORD says that we must be born again, born of water and of SPIRIT (JOHN 3:3-5); and become like little children; not that we *are* little children, but that we need to become *like* little children. "For such is the Kingdom of Heaven;" so much of what people believe hangs on a few words. I am one such person. I take the WORD *literally*. I take the leadings of the SPIRIT *seriously*. I have to; my life depends on clearly deciphering what I am being told and shown, because much of it ends up right here, in the pages you are reading; and I am accountable for every word I am writing here; accountable to my LORD JESUS CHRIST; not to any man.

Where does life begin? At what point in gestation is a child considered a human being? Consider the virgin birth of LORD JESUS. HE was conceived by the HOLY SPIRIT of FATHER GOD. I consider HIM *alive* from that point. I realize HE is Eternal; HE passed from Heaven to earth in a way that only faith can conceive of; but as far as HIS life on earth, HE was alive the moment HE was conceived. Even Elisabeth's child, when she heard Mary, LORD JESUS' mother's salutation, John the Baptist, while still in the womb, leaped for joy, and Elisabeth was filled with the HOLY SPIRIT (LUKE 1:41). This in itself tells me that a child, while still in the gestation period, is alive, and has life.

I cannot get to the place that I was hoping to get to. That is the place where I could confidently say that a child goes to Heaven if they are aborted or die moments or even days after birth. There is no evidence in the WORD of GOD, only that a child six months from conception can sense another's child while still in the womb, even though this was the LORD we are talking about. On the other hand, there is no evidence that they don't go to Heaven, only the belief of the person involved has an opinion at this point. I ultimately see in black and white; I understand how a person, particularly if they regret the death of the child, would want to believe that their child is in Heaven with LORD JESUS. There would be much peace in that feeling. But I believe what I believe, and share as I am shown. I have said it, and I stand on what I believe. If my LORD JESUS wants to change my heart in this matter, I am more than all for it. It *will* take HIS SPIRIT to do it for me.

I believe that because of the Eternal consequences, abortion should be a thing to avoid. In the case of rape or incest, there is still a child at stake, and FATHER GOD has a plan for each child; aborting only robs GOD of an opportunity to see a life to fruition; to fulfill HIS Holy perfect will through; to bless others through; and to love them. I believe that LORD JESUS *loved* those children he blessed while HE was here. HE loves each and every child that is conceived. I believe it grieves HIM to the very depths of HIS heart when one dies, for whatever the reason.

This is the end of the discussion of abortion, and the predestination of children that die at an early age. I sincerely hope that what you believe happens to these children does not cause another to stumble.

Is it ever alright to speak lies, even if it's to protect the feelings of another? You've heard the term "brutally honest?" I take it the person that is brutally honest is one that speaks the truth even when it hurts. I believe it is never alright to speak lies, for the WORD's sake. Complacency is an accomplice of lies, in that one must lower their standards to even speak or think of speaking lies. Complacency says it's alright to bend some rules, if it serves your purpose. This is a lie in itself. I hate complacency in my own life, and have come to terms with it. It must not be allowed in our lives. Confession of the presence of complacency and the sin of lying will bring about forgiveness from my LORD JESUS (if one asks for it); then comes the difficult part of facing like circumstances where lying *was* the preferred response. Heed the WORD:

> Let no corrupt communication proceed out of your mouth, but that which is good to the use of edifying, that it may minister grace unto the hearers.

> (EPHESIANS 4:29.)

I asked my LORD JESUS what was next to write about last night. HE spoke to me and told me, showing me at the same time in HIS HOLY SPIRIT, that there was more on the subject of lies that needed to be expounded upon; namely, Satan's lies and how he does this to me, and how he gains entrance *to* lie to me; all this from personal experience, and from the WORD's instruction, and the HOLY SPIRIT's insight.

Consider the SPIRIT realm: Angels everywhere; they have access to each of us, to help, and protect, and to teach us in any way that FATHER GOD sees fit. An excerpt from my first book tells of a time where my angel spoke commanding, yet comforting words to me when Satan had manifested himself to me in a most horrifying way.

It stands to reason that if angels have this kind of access, that Satan and his demons have access to us as well. I know from very real encounters that Satan knows what I am thinking. He has access to my dreams. In fact, just today, I was taking a nap and before I awoke, he had used an image of my late father in a nightmare that could have had repercussions had LORD JESUS not woke me up and led me to command Satan to stop, and leave and not come back in that way ever again, all in my LORD JESUS' Name.

The screen of my mind is a playground for satanic activity, though since my LORD JESUS delivered me from wicked imaginations; it hasn't been a problem of late. So let me tell you of the time when I had not as yet been delivered.

Wicked imaginations are an abomination to the LORD (PROVERBS 6:18); they are sin. They are sometimes called more frequently-fantasies, or daydreams. One thing is for sure-they are being fueled by Satan and his demons. The wicked imaginations that I would have were always sexual in nature. They included fornications, adultery, and covetousness. Married, or unmarried, it didn't seem to matter. All that mattered was my pleasure, and the release from everyday life. They consumed me, taking up most of my time, whether I was at work, or at home relaxing, or in bed trying to sleep. Satan didn't let up for a moment. His attacks on me were relentless (they still are, they have only changed in appearance, and intensity).

In my first book, Chosen Vessel was a true story of when wicked imaginations led FATHER GOD to judge me unworthy of HIS Kingdom. They had become so frequent, and all consuming that HE simply had enough. Read the book, it is very captivating reading.

Let's get back to how Satan gains entrance to our minds and hearts to lie to us. In me, specifically, a complacent attitude takes over; one that says it is all right to let Satan use my mind to manifest his lies. Mind you, it is not a voluntary giving of permission to Satan to use my mind; it is simply an attitude that takes me over where I am very lax as far as wanting to fight off his lies. This is a very dangerous place to be, and one that I try to dissuade from taking me over. The point is this: Satan gained entrance to my mind by me not having my guard up and in place.

Complacency is one of Satan's very effective tools. One of Webster's Collegiate Dictionary's descriptions of complacency is one of being "unconcerned." He has hidden himself, and even to those who he has revealed himself to-has deceived them into being unconcerned of the dangers of letting him have his way in their lives, and through them, affecting other's lives; namely secular TV, and movies; and music, and the media. The deception is so deep that any effort to dispel those lies will only lead to ridicule and resentment. We, as the Body of CHRIST, can only protect ourselves from the onslaught of the works of this deception.

I have prayed just now, and will continue to pray that what has been revealed in this book would not be buried by Satan, but would help those involved to see the lies and deception and seek freedom from them. Satan could easily try to steal from you what has been spoken in this book; that I have made clear, I believe. I command right now, in my LORD JESUS' Name, that Satan would not steal anything read in this book from the one reading it; in my LORD JESUS' Holy Name, I pray it.

Chapter 7

Since this book is called "Sin," my first inclination was to write about how sinning makes a Christian's life harder; leading into the other aspects of sin. The HOLY SPIRIT had other plans, and it waited till now to come out in this book. I have come to have great love and respect for the leading of the HOLY SPIRIT.

Let us consider the after effects of sinning; say the sin was not intentional, but happened out of unknown pride. 3 things could happen at this point for the Child of GOD: 1st is an easy confession to LORD JESUS and just as easy, forgiveness from HIM; all settled. 2nd, and most likely the one that happens to new Christians, and those who are repeat offenders (like me), the first reaction is one of guilt and fear, that facing an angry GOD would send you straight to Hell, when FATHER GOD is more than ready and willing, and wanting to forgive our sins, and cleanse us from all unrighteousness in the precious Blood of HIS SON, our LORD JESUS CHRIST. Add the condemnation from Satan that makes it even more difficult to come to our FATHER in LORD JESUS' Name, and you have a situation where being forgiven means even more to the person who committed the sin(s). An attitude of great thankfulness comes from their hearts toward FATHER GOD and LORD JESUS.

3rd, and most regrettable, is the reaction out of apathy and complacency. "Oh, it doesn't matter; I will deal with it later." A sin left unconfessed, and unforgiven will snowball into other sins later on. I for one, *have* to come to the FATHER and confess my sin. If I don't, HE allows Satan to condemn me so powerfully that I can't move; any direction I try to go is like walking through thick mud. The last thing I want is for GOD to allow me to go on, without being forgiven. Praise *be* to FATHER GOD for HIS Goodness, which leads me to come to HIM in repentance, seeking HIS forgiveness for the sins that I have committed.

Now all this that was just talked about was of an incidental sin; but what about the ones committed like mine that have been done intentionally? One thing is for certain, the condemnation is stronger from Satan. Pride plays a big part in sins committed willfully. To the unknowledgeable, even the WORD can be a source of condemnation. Take HEBREWS 10: 26-31 for example. Satan would love to convince me that every time I sin willfully I am bound for the Lake. But I can't help thinking about what it says:

> For if we sin willfully after that we have received the knowledge of the truth, there remaineth no more sacrifice for sins, but a certain fearful looking for of judgment and fiery indignation, which shall devour the adversaries.
>
> (HEBREWS 10: 26,27.)

And:

> Of how much sorer punishment, suppose ye, shall he be thought worthy, who hath trodden underfoot the SON of GOD, and hath counted the blood of the covenant, wherewith he was sanctified, an unholy thing, and hath done despite unto the SPIRIT of Grace? For we know HIM who hath said, Vengeance *belongeth* unto ME, I will recompence, saith the LORD. And again, the LORD shall judge HIS people. *It is* a fearful thing to fall into the hands of the living GOD.
>
> (HEBREWS 10: 29-31.)

Taking the whole chapter into context, instead of just reading these words, (for all of us have a tendency to sin, whether willfully or not); the point is, why then would LORD JESUS say in MATTHEW 6:12, when HE was teaching us the how to pray to the FATHER, "…and forgive us our debts, as we forgive our debtors," if we didn't have a tendency to sin? Or that of MATTHEW 6: 14,15:

"For if you forgive men their trespasses, your Heavenly FATHER will also forgive you: but if you forgive not men their trespasses, neither will your FATHER forgive your trespasses."

(MATTHEW 6:14,15.)

Sounds to me that LORD JESUS and the FATHER know the tendencies of the hearts of men and women; they know that we sin, and have provided guidance for what to do when we do. There are clear guidelines of what the truth of the matter is:

For the wages of sin *is* death; but the gift of GOD *is* eternal life through JESUS CHRIST our LORD.

(ROMANS 6:23.)

My LORD wants me to talk about *my* sins. I just asked HIM, and that is what HE told me. Closer to me than my own breath, HE is; and HE knows my every move, for it was HIS FATHER that planned out my whole life long before anything was ever created. HE has a special Grace for me, knowing that I have an unfortunate tendency to sin. I am better than I was yesterday, though; each day that I face the temptations of Satan I get stronger and stronger in resisting him. The choices I make throughout the day are dependent on what I feel for my LORD JESUS; love and a deep respect for what HE is accomplishing in my life, through HIS HOLY SPIRIT.

Waking up each morning is a tremendous blessing; and I praise my LORD JESUS for getting me through the night's dreams. I believe that some of my sins come from what Satan plants in my subconscious during the night. I praise my LORD for monitoring my dreams, letting Satan plant only what HE wants me to deal with through this time. Sexual dreams, or dreams that have a sexual overtone to them help me to identify problem areas in my own conscious. I wake up and realize that I can't remember what was in my dreams; hoping that something that doesn't belong in me hasn't been planted in me. Then LORD JESUS shows me that HE is, and was there through the night, inside me, seeing what was dreamed first hand. Like I said, HE monitors the whole night's proceedings.

As I pray in the morning, before I do anything else, I am instructed by what is prayed for what I should expect during that day; mostly right now is the blessing upon what I am writing, which you are reading right now. Any sins committed during the writing of this book have only served to enrichen its content. What I endure, what I experience is all written in this book, and in the other two books that I have written. If you haven't read them yet, I encourage you to do so. Chosen Vessel, and Changing Vessel, are the names of them; they are available in E-book fashion as well.

There is a measure of pride in me as I sin willfully; it comes from believing that I can always confess my sins and be forgiven; this to me, as I think about it now, is taking strict advantage of my LORD and FATHER. I confess right now this pride and the evil thoughts that are in me. I also confess taking advantage of YOU both, in thinking this way. Please forgive me, my LORD JESUS; and thank-YOU for YOUR forgiveness, in YOUR Name, my Holy LORD JESUS.

There is a definite blessing in following the WORD, where it says:

Blessed *is* the man that endureth temptation: for when he is tried, he shall receive the crown of life, which the LORD hath promised to them that love HIM.

(JAMES 1:12.)

I have experienced this blessing before, and it is a present blessing; as in blessed *is* the man; everything is blessed; from the getting up in the morning, to the prayers throughout the day, to the relationships that

I have, to my finances; especially my relationship with my LORD and FATHER. I find an ease in the writing of this book; an ease in which the words flow out of me like rivers of living water.

In this preceding verse is a wealth of truth, and information to benefit those who look for it. First are the words "blessed *is;*" the LORD *blesses* me when I endure the temptations that Satan brings into my life. That's not to say that HE curses me when I disobey; HE merely chastises me, as any good father would do to their child. And the word "*is*" in italics denotes a present state of blessedness, all encompassing. To read this verse encourages me to *want* to resist, if only to receive the blessing. But read on: "For when he is tried…" tells me that we are immersed in temptations at times to strengthen us, and to receive the prize of the crown of life. "Which the LORD hath promised to them that love HIM;" this is perhaps my most prized of all the WORD. It tells me that if I love HIM, (and I do), that I will resist the temptations of Satan and obey the commandments and HIS WORD. I have struggled with this all my adult life; if I love my LORD, and FATHER, I *would* obey them. Satan has had a field day with me on this. "You obviously don't love them, because you keep sinning." "You love me; because I give you the things that make you feel good." All lies; and all targeted at trying to make me walk away in shame from my LORD and FATHER. I tell you he is relentless in attacking me. But praise be to my LORD JESUS, and my Holy Heavenly FATHER for their Grace and their Mercy upon me; keeping me close by their side. My angel hovering over me, and walking beside me, (even when I sin), to protect me; I will shake his mighty hand the day I am taken Home, and apologize profusely for what he had to put up with in taking care of me throughout this life.

I urge you to walk in the blessedness of resisting temptations. Join me in saying "no" to Satan when he provides an "easy ride," when we know for a truth that walking and talking LORD JESUS is not an easy way; especially in these, the "last days," when everyone is seeking their own and not the things of the LORD JESUS. Make your FATHER proud of you by obeying HIS commandments. I have received a transforming attitude adjustment as I write these words. My Holy LORD JESUS has had Mercy upon me. I praise YOU, my LORD JESUS!

Chapter 8

As I go through the day, my LORD JESUS will feed me with the subjects to be in this book. I would now like to speak about another sensitive subject (this book is filled with them, no?) It is the sad truth that Satan attacks through us; he steals through us, and destroys through us; what is our responsibility in all of this?

What are you talking about, you may ask? I have the LORD JESUS in my heart. How could Satan do *anything* through me? Consider that we are open vessels for the spirit realm to work through; the mouth and tongue are a mighty way in which he does this. The WORD says:

Death and life *are* in the power of the tongue: and they that love it shall eat the fruit thereof.

(PROVERBS 18:21.)

Think about it for a moment: to speak death includes our *own* death; the WORD says again:

"But I say unto you, that every idle word that men shall speak, they shall give account thereof in the Day of Judgment. For by thy words thou shalt be justified, and by thy words thou shalt be condemned."

(MATTHEW 12:36,37.)

Don't be deceived into a lull of apathy at our adversary, the Devil. He is very much seeking whom he may devour (1st PETER 5:8), and will steal, kill and destroy any way in which he can accomplish it. If he can get you to believe even the smallest of lies, he can (and is) speaking through you. If he can sow even the smallest thread of pride in you, you will judge your brothers and sisters unjustly, and end up him stealing their peace and love for you. That same thread of pride has a long list of stolen items with it. If he can, he will even steal from you the truth that he is able to do these things right as you read this. Do you find that your thoughts are taking you away from what you are reading? That is Satan coming to steal from you. Don't be alarmed, just calmly tell him in LORD JESUS' Name to leave, and steal nothing you are reading. It's that easy. The truth is that Satan will steal anything from the WORD, and anything pertaining to himself that would reveal him to you if you don't understand it; therefore the confusing thoughts that come into your mind when you are reading this.

Let me use the analogy of the frog in boiling water. If we, as the Body of CHRIST were to suddenly, and for the first time, land on this earth as it is right now, we would jump out of the boiling water immediately. But we have been sitting in this water from the early days of our youth, and have become complacent to the lies and tactics of our enemy. Even to the point of not recognizing him when he attacks. Therefore I am writing this book, and doing my job of revealing our enemy to you and how he does what he does.

The WORD says in MATTHEW 12:34 that out of the abundance of the heart, so speaks the mouth. Our hearts need to be filled with compassion for our brothers and sisters, first in CHRIST JESUS, and then for the lost. Ask LORD JESUS that our hearts be filled with the treasures of compassion and love for each other and that any death in our words would be forgiven and gotten rid of.

Another lie of Satan that LORD JESUS just showed me, is that of asking for things for ourselves; how else can one be outfitted for battle if one doesn't ask for the pieces of armor and their sword? How else can one be trained for battle with our enemy if one does not ask for the training? It's alright to ask for things for yourself; you ask for things for others, right? Only you can defend your ground, your family, your finances, your very peace. All are at stake in this game of life and death in the power of the tongue.

> If any man among you seems to be religious, and does not bridle his tongue but deceives his own heart, this one's religion *is* useless.

> (JAMES 1:26.)

And again:

> Even so the tongue is a little member and boasts great things. See how great a forest a little fire kindles! And the tongue *is* a fire, a world of iniquity. The tongue is so set among our members that it defiles the whole body, and sets on fire the course of nature; and it is set on fire by Hell. For every kind of beast and bird, of reptile and creature of the sea, is tamed and has been tamed by mankind. But no man can tame the tongue. *It is* an unruly evil, full of deadly poison.

> (JAMES 3: 5-8.)

Satan uses this tongue to separate us from one another. Different beliefs, instead of the one true faith in LORD JESUS CHRIST; I just had a huge case of déjà vu, that I have written these words before. Like it has been spoken to me in the past, FATHER GOD was going to show me things before they happen, just so I couldn't say that I had anything to do with bringing them to pass. I believe this book is one of those things. Praise GOD!

Different beliefs and harsh and unwarranted words of hatred and bitterness tearing at our unity; selfishness that has us thinking only of ourselves instead of taking care of our family in CHRIST JESUS; these are the painful truths of the condition of HIS Body.

Our responsibility in keeping Satan at bay, is first to keep a watch on our tongues. We cannot tame them, but we can watch what and when we say things; keeping always positive things on the tip of our tongues. Also watching out for Satan's attacks in the form of thoughts that come into our minds that we automatically respond to, thinking that they are our own. Have you ever wondered why you would think something like that? Or where did *that* thought come from? My guess would have to be Satan, if it was something perverted or unholy. It could even be something totally neutral in nature, but came at a time when you needed to be concentrating on something serious, like reading the WORD, or praying to the Holy FATHER. This is why I have always said, when you are reading the WORD, pray that the WORD would remain in your hearts and minds unchanged, undistorted, unperverted, and *unstolen* by Satan; because if he catches you not understanding something, it *will* be stolen from you. Satan does not want you to ingest the living WORD, much less understand it, and act upon it in your life. But praise FATHER GOD and our LORD JESUS that they are in control. What does that mean in a world that is seems to be spinning *out* of control? Let's talk about just what FATHER GOD and LORD JESUS *are* in control of.

Destiny; predestination, and the fulfilling of the will of GOD; I was once shown an image of GOD sitting upon HIS Throne, deciding all the details of creation from the beginning of creation to Eternity with HIS Children in Heaven; every last detail. This includes all of the choices that we will ever make in our lives; even the fall of man, and Lucifer being found with iniquity in him, being cast out of Heaven; I believe it is all a part of HIS big plan, and that we are merely living out our daily lives to the fulfilling of FATHER GOD's Holy perfect will. Then why do I pray for HIS will to be done in earth as it is in Heaven each morning? Because of Satan stealing GOD's will out of our lives. But then, isn't that a part of HIS perfect plan, too? Everything that Satan does is directed by LORD JESUS, for HE *is* KING over all creation. I believe LORD JESUS allows Satan to do his dirty work to fulfill the requirements of the destiny of planet earth, from the Antichrist, to the final judgments on those who have the Mark of the Beast; all of which were predestined to have it. How could a GOD that is love predestine anyone to burn in the LAKE of FIRE forever? What if HE chose, while sitting on HIS Throne, for your child to burn? How could HE do that? Many would say, because HE is GOD, don't question the Almighty. PROVERBS 16:4 says:

> The LORD hath made all *things* for Himself: yea even the wicked for the day of evil.
>
> (PROVERBS 16:4.)

What can you say to that? I know that GOD *is* love, and that LORD JESUS died on the cross out of love for us, to be the propitiation for our sins. I know that it says in the WORD that FATHER GOD would that none should perish, but all come to repentance:

> The LORD is not slack concerning HIS promise, as some men count slackness; but is longsuffering to us-ward, not willing that any should perish, but that all should come to repentance.
>
> (2nd PETER 3:9.)

I beg YOUR forgiveness Holy FATHER, for responding like Job. I just know that there are people who wonder about these things; and I thought that writing it out would come to an understanding that everyone could live with; namely YOUR truth. Again, I beg YOUR forgiveness in YOUR Name, my LORD JESUS.

I know that FATHER GOD and LORD JESUS don't want anything to be stolen from you. They want you to fulfill FATHER GOD's holy perfect will in your lives; and *are* moving each of us in that direction. This is one of the things I am praying for the Body of CHRIST each morning. The only things that stand in the way of these things coming to pass are our own sins, and attitudes of selfishness and unforgiveness in our hearts. So let's confess these things and be forgiven, forgiving those in our lives that have sinned against us, and move on!

Reading back over this I was given something to write in the midst of what was already written; just that quick, it was stolen from me. I had tried just for a second to understand what was being lead to write, and poof! It was gone just like that. LORD JESUS then led me to command

Satan to replace what was stolen with that which was taken from me at that moment, all in LORD JESUS' Name. I have to say that I know what it's like; and I know by the leading of the HOLY SPIRIT just what to do in case it does happen. It is this that I want to impart to you, who are reading this now. You are not alone in your confusion, it is merely an attack. Praise FATHER GOD for LORD JESUS' Name, in which we can and must command Satan and his demons back away from the Body of CHRIST; and be the spotless and blameless Children of GOD that HE wants and will have us to be.

How does Satan steal through us? Again, primarily through the answer of the tongue; stealing each other's peace and joy by our constant complaining and gossiping, which he plants in our minds and hearts. I have been guilty of this in my time; and it is only by the precious HOLY SPIRIT's conviction that I am even aware I am doing it. We need to praise FATHER GOD and LORD JESUS for their HOLY SPIRIT! Now I need to tell you of a truth that is somewhat difficult to tell. While the Devil is on this earth, he is seeking whom he may devour; this we all should know. But what we may not know is the way in which he devours; or steals, kills and destroys. His primary target when it comes to our lives is our faith; the faith that we have in our LORD JESUS. If he could, he would steal our salvation right out from under us. Again, Satan stole what I was just given to write; but Glory! For my Holy LORD JESUS, who gave it right back to me when I was allowed to realize it *had* been stolen from me. Please allow me to re-iterate:

> Put on the whole armor of GOD, that you may be able to stand against the wiles of the Devil.
>
> (EPHESIANS 6:11.)

When Satan tries to steal our faith, it is our own shield of faith that we must use in defense. Satan doesn't need to steal when we don't fully understand the leading of the HOLY SPIRIT; for he knows that we won't act upon partial information, first out of guilt, (which Satan plants at that moment you realize you don't understand all of what was given by the HOLY SPIRIT); and second, out of fear that we will miss something that FATHER GOD has for us to do; both paralyzing emotions. If we move at that moment to re-receive what it was, then comes the Devil and steals, or tries to steal by blocking your mind with thoughts that are not your own. I told you it was difficult. Satan isn't a quaint enemy. He is powerful, and sly, and deceptive. And he will steal and destroy through you if you allow him to. The leading I was just given by LORD JESUS was this: to start the day by commanding Satan to steal and destroy <u>nothing</u> this day in your own life and that of your flock; all in LORD JESUS' Holy Name.

There is of course the physical realm of theft, and stealing. Satan convinces a person to do the act of theft (or any number of other illegal or immoral things) all the while remaining hidden from the person's view by being in the spirit realm; if a person listens to the lies and deceit and chooses to act upon what was planted in them, they do those things. If it is Satan's desire that you be caught at what *he* desired you to do, so much more the glee you give Satan.

If Satan wanted you to steal or destroy another's property, or person, he would first prep you to be susceptible to receiving his lies about what he wanted you to accomplish for him. Then after he had prepped you, he would then plant the seeds of the unrighteous act within you, calling upon his other followers to fertilize and water those plants of unrighteousness. Let me give you examples: say Satan wanted to cause you to commit the act of rape; first, hypothetically, he would have you raised by a family that had no respect for women; prepping you with abuse or neglect, planting the seeds of loneliness in you. When you were the age of acting upon the lies of Satan, he would then create the need for self satisfaction, and wicked imaginations, or an unrealistic fantasy life of unreachable relationships. The lies of Satan might go like this: I want what I cannot have; therefore I will take what I cannot have. The seeds of raping another are planted; and since they were prepped so well with loneliness, they believe the lies of Satan, and think it is all inside of them, *of* them. Who argues with themselves, except those who question the source of the voice inside of them?

Again, I am not saying that everyone who grows up in an abusive family will turn out to be rapists. Come on-use your GOD given sense;

it's just that, hypothetically, Satan uses like circumstances to promote the evil he does through people that listen to his lies. I tell you, Satan has hid himself deep in the guise of self, convincing people to do all kinds of wicked things, thinking that they are doing it of themselves. Then there are those who openly say that the Devil told them to do what they did, and we write it off as delusion.

This brings up another interesting aspect of Satan' voice in our lives; we live in a three dimensional world; but even though we walk through this life, we are still within earshot of the spirit realm. Satan's voice inside our heads, in the form of thoughts and in my case, his actual voice, shows me that we are indeed attached to the spirit realm, or at the very least, accessible to it. When we command Satan in LORD JESUS' Name, he hears us and obeys, because LORD JESUS has defeated him.

It is FATHER GOD's mercy that delivers people from these like circumstances and brings them face to face with HIS SON, bringing them into the Kingdom of my LORD JESUS. It is not everyone that is delivered, for this depends on people praying for them; and as the WORD says:

For HE saith to Moses, I will have mercy on whom I will have mercy, and I will have compassion on whom I will have compassion. So then *it is* not of him that willeth, not of him that runneth, but of GOD that showeth mercy.

(ROMANS 9:15,16.)

And again:

Therefore hath HE mercy on whom HE will *have mercy,* and whom HE will HE hardeneth.

(ROMANS 9:18.)

I worship my Holy Heavenly FATHER, for HIS exceeding abundant mercy upon me; to my knowledge HE has never hardened my heart;

even in the light of people doing evil things to me. HE has led me to do as the WORD says, and pray for those which despitefully use you (MATTHEW 5: 44).

Our enemy wants to steal permanently, but praise FATHER GOD and our LORD JESUS that they give back what is stolen; unless they know we won't do anything with that which was given, missing an opportunity to glorify GOD, and further the Kingdom of our LORD JESUS CHRIST. Many are called, few are chosen; it says in the WORD (MATTHEW 22:14). If one person will not use what FATHER GOD gives, HE will give it to another with the same gift. The WORD says:

"For whosoever hath, to him shall be given, and he shall have more abundance: but whosoever hath not, from him shall be taken away even that he hath."

(MATTHEW 13:12.)

Most everyone has done, or experienced my next subject. I had been caught up in it for many years, till my Holy Heavenly FATHER told me the next time I did it I would die! HE said it in a very plain, noncoersive fashion; and I believe HIM. I had tried at one time after HIM telling me this to do it, and guess what happened? Before I could accomplish anything, the electricity went out for a moment, and the phone voice told of a power outage. *Immediately* when I tried; I have not tried since, it scared me so much to realize just how serious my FATHER is about adultery and covetousness, and wicked imaginations. The WORD says again:

Now the works of the flesh are manifest, which are *these*; Adultery, fornication, uncleanness, lasciviousness, idolatry, witchcraft, hatred, variance, emulations, wrath, strife, seditions, heresies, envying, murders, drunkenness, revellings, and such like, of the which I tell you before, and have told you in time past, that they which do such things shall not inherit the Kingdom of GOD.

(GALATIANS 5:19-21.)

That's why FATHER GOD is so adamant about me stopping these things. What about after you become a Child of GOD? I have done some of these things, including the covetousness and wicked imaginations several times, and have repented of such things in my life, being forgiven of them on numerous occasions. Once forgiven, it *is* forgotten. Praise GOD!

Wicked imaginations, which follow heavily in the mind and heart, are an abomination to the LORD (PROVERBS 6:18), with the end result of this act allowing Satan to steal physical integrity, closeness with your partner, and with others; he steals confidence, and the presence of the HOLY SPIRIT will back away when it is used. If left unconfessed and unforgiven, it will snowball into allowing Satan access to the body you are in, planting seeds of all kinds of unrighteousness. In my own life, wicked imaginations had led to the sins of drinking alcohol; like the proverbial cigarette after sex; a feeling of narcissistic behavior was taking over, and only by the conviction of the HOLY SPIRIT have I come to be rid of both desires. I should say the desire is sometimes still there, but I do not act upon it. Deep depression is another problem that accompanies drinking of alcohol; I have dealt with this as well, and am happy to say that I am free of all drinking with the exception of a little red wine occasionally for my heart's sake; and even this is being convicted by the HOLY SPIRIT to stop, the WORD saying:

> Be not drunk with wine, whe1re in is excess, but be filled with the SPIRIT.
>
> (EPHESIANS 5:18.)

Since the body is the Temple of the HOLY SPIRIT (1ˢᵗ CORINTHIANS 6:19,20), I believe touching this body in an unholy and unpure way is sin. I do not want to grieve the HOLY SPIRIT of FATHER GOD ((EPHESIANS 4:30).

Right now I want to speak something that is truly important to my heart.

It is not my intent to condemn in *any* way. It is only the purpose of this book to enlighten those who are of the Body of CHRIST, and may know of people who are battling with these circumstances. I love each and every one of you in my LORD JESUS CHRIST. I am led to seek the unity of the Body of CHRIST, as the WORD says:

> With all lowliness and meekness, with longsuffering, forbearing one another in love; endeavoring to keep the unity of the SPIRIT in the bond of peace. *There is* one Body, and one SPIRIT, even as you are called in one hope of your calling; one LORD, one faith, and baptism, One GOD and FATHER of all, who *is* above all, and through all, and in you all.
>
> (EPHESIANS 4:2-6.)

Demon possession was clearly prevalent in the time that LORD JESUS was on this earth. I believe that demons can't die, for they will spend Eternity in the Lake of Fire, so even if they inhabited a person till they died, they would simply leave that body and seek someone else to inhabit. Demon possession is nearly unheard of in this day and age; it really makes me wonder, if they are still here on this earth, where are they? What are they doing? Who have they inhabited? If there are demon possessed people around, why don't we recognize them as such? Has the deception of Satan blinded our eyes from seeing possession as it is? It says in the WORD that one third of the angels of Heaven were swept away by Satan to become demons, and cast them to the earth (REVELATION 12:3-9), so we know they are here; and with the power of Satan at their disposal, their main purpose is to do his bidding.

> And when HE had called unto HIM HIS twelve disciples, HE gave them power *against* unclean spirits, to cast them out, and to heal all manner of sickness and all manner of disease.
>
> (MATTHEW 10:1.)

Unclean spirits, or demons; as opposed to "clean" ones, or angels which are ministering spirits; I believe we are to perform these very same functions, that of casting out demons. One would have to ask LORD JESUS to confirm the gift of discernment; for you couldn't just walk up to a person and start an exorcism. Not in this day and age; I don't even know how one would do such a thing; it would have to be totally lead by LORD JESUS, like the one mentioned in my first book. I guess I do know how; I have cast out a demon from one of my friends. I am still horrified at the soulless black eyes that the demon had as it looked out of her eyes. Another time, I was face to face with a demon in another of my close friends, only that time I did nothing to cast it out. I regret that very much. I haven't seen my friend for a number of years. I still wonder how his life would have been changed if that demon had been cast out. While we were standing there, face to face, it's like the demon was hovering over him, through him, flexing his muscles; so to speak, daring me to do anything, which he already knew somehow that I wouldn't. My friend just stood there, with a helpless look on his face. I can still see it just like it was yesterday, and that was probably 20 years ago.

Is demon possession a thing of the past? I believe it isn't. There are certain characteristics of certain people that lead me to believe they have an infestation of demons upon, or in them. The demons themselves have facial characteristics, and mannerisms that, when in a person, differentiate themselves from those who don't have demons. The more evil a demon is, the more aggressively they take over a person; and the aggression that person shows toward others, and themselves, is dependent upon this as well. Have you ever met a person that, well, something just wanted to jump out at you from inside them? Or say, something was calling you from inside them, that you knew wasn't the SPIRIT of FATHER GOD? Something that just made your skin *crawl?* I have numerous times. And I account for this demon activity. There are demons that make a person seclude themselves, edging them ever so slowly towards suicide; I was again, one of those persons. And there again, are demons who want to get others to join them, causing the persons who are infested with them to commit fornication with themselves; demons of lust, and unnatural affection, for example. That's definitely not to say that everyone who commits fornication is possessed; it's just that I believe those who are, are more prone to it.

It was just pointed out to me that it is questionable that there are different degrees of wickedness; different intensities of evil. I believe that the more demons that a person has will cause the infested to be more aggressive, like in MATTHEW 8:28-34:

> And when HE was come to the other side into the country of the Gergesenes, there met HIM two possessed with devils, coming out of the tombs, exceeding fierce, so that no man might pass by that way. And, behold, they cried out, saying what have we to do with thee, JESUS, thou SON of GOD? Art thou come hither to torment us before the time? And there was a good way off from them an herd of many swine feeding. So the devils besought HIM, saying, if thou cast us out, suffer us to do away into the herd of swine. And HE said to them, go. And when they were come out, they went into the herd of swine: and behold, the whole herd of swine ran violently down a steep place into the sea and perished in the waters.
>
> (MATTHEW 8: 28-32.)

Then there are possessions by a single demon that only prayer and fasting will remove them (MATTHEW 17:15-21), making me believe that these demons are of a more evil design. My point is that, on the other hand, there are angels of varying degrees of power as told in REVELATION:

> And after these things I saw another angel come down from Heaven, having great power; and the earth was lightened with his glory.
>
> (REVELATION 18:1.)

If then, there are varying degrees of power in angels in Heaven, I believe there are varying degrees of wickedness in the demons on this earth. It was also pointed out to me that the more evil a demon is, the more abominable the sins committed in the person they inhabit. Sin is sin, in FATHER GOD's eyes. Only we, as the human race, recognize sins of a varying degree; somewhat similar to the justice system condemning the act of murder more than that of running a stop sign. I'm not saying that we should judge all infractions of the law by death or life in prison; I'm saying that as far as sin is concerned, GOD has judged sin once and for all in the cross of my LORD JESUS CHRIST. LORD JESUS took *all* of the sins of the world and took them to death with HIM (1ˢᵗ JOHN 2:2), and (JOHN 1:29). We, as the Body of CHRIST, need to see sin as FATHER GOD sees it; forgivable, and do our part to see those that are being infested with the demons of Satan set free and then on to be Children of the Most High.

This next verse is one of my favorites, for it tells of demons:

"When the unclean spirit is gone out of a man, he walks through dry places, seeking rest, and finds none. Then he says, I will return into my house from whence I came out; and when he come, he finds *it* empty, swept, and garnished. Then goes he and takes with himself seven other spirits more wicked than himself, and they enter in and dwell there: and the last *state* of that man is worse than the first.

(MATTHEW 12:43-45.)

Looking into these verses, there is a wealth of insights and knowledge to be gleaned from it. To begin with, when LORD JESUS cast out demons, he must have done something to prevent them from being reinfested with them; I just can't believe that he would leave them to be attacked again and let eight demons enter again after casting one out. LORD JESUS led me to pray for the HOLY SPIRIT to enter my friend when the demon was cast out of her. Where does the demon go, seeking rest? Does he just walk around aimlessly, undirected, and then when he can't find any rest, *then* he goes back to the person he was in? The legion of demons that were in the man in MARK 5:1-19, sought LORD JESUS to send them into a herd of pigs. When all the pigs choked in the water, did they go find someone else to enter? It doesn't say; but it makes sense. Death seems to free them up to inhabit others; death or being cast out.

"Verily, verily, I say unto you, he that believeth on ME, the works that I do he shall do also; and greater *works* than these shall he do; because I go unto MY FATHER."

(JOHN 14:12.)

The very presence of demons causes a reaction out of people; for example, the demon of lust causes the loins to react; the demons of unnatural affection cause nervousness in most people who have made up their minds about their own sexuality, for it questions their stand on such issues; the demons of hatred bring about the reactions that open hostility cause, and so on.

And what about the people who are found to be possessed? If we *knew*, how would we treat them? Not as a criminal, from a spiritual standpoint; but necessarily they would have to be held accountable for any crimes committed, even though they were known to be possessed. I believe that only those of the Body of CHRIST can and should deal with the spiritual aspects of a person found to be infested or "surrounded" by demons; commanding them away and out of the person in LORD JESUS' Name, giving the glory of it to the Holy FATHER, in LORD JESUS' Name.

An interesting fact, one that I cannot explain, is that when I was unmedicated as far as my schizophrenia goes, Satan fed me with all kinds of information about him (it could have been the HOLY SPIRIT, at the time I couldn't tell them apart-that was back in the 80's, and I was very afflicted) and his demons. I heard Satan's voice quite frequently. Then I was introduced to the V.A. and they put me on Haldol. For the first time in my adult life, I had *no voices*. Everything that I had come to know was taken away by a medicine! Talk about life changing; but not in a good way; all that I knew had become a lie and all the papers that I wrote on the subject of Satan and his demons was put by the wayside. I had to come off the Haldol for the side effects reason. The voices returned with a vengeance, only then I had to come face to face with my illness that the voices were coming from inside of *me*.

Was Satan's voice real? Why did the medicine take it away from me? Does Satan speak to those who have schizophrenia? Those were the questions that I was asking myself, with no answers coming forthwith. Interestingly enough, my word count at the point of "forthwith" was 15,666. I had to laugh at that, though the mark of the beast is *not* funny.

One thing more, I am not saying that everyone who utilizes self pleasure will be afflicted by the demons of Satan; it is merely one way in which Satan gains access to the bodies we are in; just as demon possession is. It is of course a private matter, between partners, or close friends. There are millions of opinions on each of these subjects, and who's to say which the right ones are. Mine are just one of the millions; I just have the leading of the HOLY SPIRIT to write about them.

Opinions on sin vary with the individual; I prefer to go by the WORD of GOD. One of the most difficult of verses is that of 1ˢᵗ JOHN 3:9:

Whosoever is born of GOD doth not sin; for his seed remaineth in him: and he cannot sin, because he is born of GOD.

(1ˢᵗ JOHN 3:9)

These are some of the strongest words spoken in the Bible, and ones that people (including myself) tend to fall under condemnation from Satan for. It is the basis for my decision to stop the self pleasure. It is also the basis for my view that we can and will be virtually sinless before the second coming of our LORD JESUS; at least the sins committed willfully. Now I have been a Child of GOD for almost 26 years, and am just now coming to the point of letting go of the sins of my past (regrets included). So what about those that just come into the Kingdom, and have all the baggage of their old nature? The answer is that the HOLY SPIRIT will begin work in them, just as he does in each of FATHER GOD's Children when they come to LORD JESUS and ask HIM into their hearts. I believe that as long as you are trying, you are ok. The WORD says:

Being confident of this very thing, that HE which hath begun a good work in you will perform *it* until the day of JESUS CHRIST.

(PHILIPPIANS 1:6.)

Praise FATHER GOD for HIS wonderful Goodness; HE is leading in these last days a mighty revival of souls in repentance unto HIMSELF through HIS SON, LORD JESUS CHRIST. Those who have been deceived will find the true path back to the Throne of Grace in HIS Mercy, to be forgiven, and shown the correct way to live this life, as I have been.

The WORD says:

Now the SPIRIT speaketh expressly, that in the latter times some shall depart from the faith, giving heed to seducing spirits, and the doctrines of devils; speaking lies in hypocrisy; having their conscience seared with a hot iron;

(1st TIMOTHY 4:1.)

I believe we are in those latter times. The only thing that can deliver us from these deceiving spirits *is the* HOLY SPIRIT of our LORD JESUS CHRIST; I pray each morning for the manifestation of the fruit of the SPIRIT in our lives, and to be an overcomer over the fruit of the flesh and all that is an abomination to the LORD. I receive it for us in LORD JESUS' Name.

Chapter 9

Music has two sources: selfish, or GODLY-and it's who the music glorifies that defines the two. Even if the music is neutral, such as classical music, it still has a source of inspiration; there is no fence sitting in this world, it either glorifies FATHER GOD and LORD JESUS, or it glorifies self. The spirit behind the music is what I am talking about; or should I say SPIRIT, for the music that is GODLY in nature. I would like to talk about the dangers of listening to certain types of music; and the definite danger of singing along with the words; for there is permanence in the spoken word. Even if you don't sing along with the music, it still enters into your conscious and subconscious mind.

Music that I have listened to (and sang along with at one time or another) that is secular in nature, I have been shown that Satan uses it to reinforce in its listeners the refusal to obey the WORD of GOD; rebellion would be the word to describe it. The WORD says that rebellion *is as the* sin of witchcraft, and stubbornness *is as* iniquity and idolatry (1ˢᵗ SAMUEL 15:23). I know of more than one song that promotes being "alive," and the joys of being "alive." Now the WORD says:

For you are dead, and your life is hid with CHRIST in GOD.

(COLOSSIANS 3:3.)

It could, and has been taken as a play on words, but the spirit behind the words in Satan's eyes is that it argues with and plants seeds of refusing to heed and obey the WORD; the truth of it anyway. If you are singing the words I'm staying alive, you are directly opposing the truth that you are dead, and dead to sin. Even if you are not yet a Child of GOD and sing this, it still reinforces the fact that you are alive, and not "dead, "as we all should be per the WORD of GOD.

The act of Satan through self is a point of contention in some people; their point being that self has nothing to do with Satan, when I believe it does. When we were created (Adam, that is), GOD breathed into Adam's nostrils the breath of life and he became a living soul (GENESIS 2:7); now being unaware of one's own nakedness is a very good sign that you are not self aware. Neither Adam nor Eve was aware that they were naked up to the time that they disobeyed GOD and ate of the fruit of the Tree of the Knowledge of Good and Evil. Once their eyes were opened, they became self aware, and knowledgeable of their own nakedness. It was then that Satan started to feed their "selves," and act through them, such as the case of Cain and Able, where the first case of Satan destroying a life by murder came about (GENESIS 4:8).

I was just told by the counsel of my son that my target audience is the Christian community, and that those who read this won't be the ones that listen to secular music; but in the same breath, they probably know of someone who does, and it is my hope to enlighten those to the dangers of certain types of music; and especially the dangers of the permanence of the spoken word in singing along with that music.

The secular music that I still listen to helps me to spot the lies and deceit of Satan in the music he has created through those that have listened to him through their "selves." It helps me to realize the patterns of sin in my own life; which brings me to my next subject: the perversion of our memories by the music that we listen to. Have you ever noticed that your memories have been challenged by a song playing in your ears or in your mind? Secular music especially; Satan knows what you are remembering when a song comes into your thoughts. It is an attack on your memories. What you remember can be vague at best, especially in me; and if our enemy wants to change a pattern of thought by changing an aspect of a distant, (but still relative) memory, he will do it. Another way he changes thought patterns is through dreams. I have been led to confess sins done in dreams, which a friend of mine says is not necessary. My LORD JESUS and my FATHER GOD tells me that I need to. I choose to believe them, not taking the chance of having unconfessed sin in my life. Many times I have awakened from a dream not realizing just what has happened in the dream; all I can remember is that something has been altered. A relationship turned bad, or made worse because of an argument in the dream; it is my responsibility to command Satan at the point of recognition that something has been changed by him. It is because my LORD JESUS is there with me in my dreams as well, that I am even aware that something has changed. My word count once again is 16,666. It has no bearing on what is being written, I just thought I'd mention that.

The power that Satan wields through music is staggering; especially in these, the last days when people are begging for answers through their music. Most answer themselves, by planting seeds of doubt in the WORD of GOD, or in GOD Himself; they promote fornication and lust in place of real love (which *is* GOD); they talk about real life circumstances, and put the blame on people instead of the person who is responsible-Satan, and his demons. Now it comes to me that we are responsible for our own choices, but who gave those choices to us? If it was the Devil, we must acknowledge and blame him; if it was FATHER GOD who gave us the choices, it is our own that we will be blaming, and dealing with the condemnation from our enemy, Satan, alongside it; for we didn't do what GOD wanted us to do. If we are in CHRIST JESUS, there is no more condemnation, for we walk after the SPIRIT, and not after the flesh (ROMANS 8:1); meaning that the music we listen to is of GOD, and glorifies HIM. For the sake of examples to write about, I still listen to some of the old nature things. I *have* deleted some music from my library for its offensiveness, and seed planting capabilities, through the leading of the HOLY SPIRIT. After the writing of this book, in the time I am given, I will probably delete more.

I not saying that people who write secular music are listening directly to Satan; what I am saying is that Satan uses self to tempt people into writing music which does not glorify FATHER GOD. If you are writing music, particularly the words of the songs, be careful what you use as your inspiration; for even as there are billions of things to use as inspiration, there are only two main sources; FATHER GOD/LORD JESUS, and self; and Satan may disguise himself through self to deceive you. Please be very careful.

Again, it is not my intention to condemn anyone. Enlighten, yes; for the wiles of the Devil are to be revealed so we may walk in safety in this world of sin and rebellion. Wise as serpents and harmless as doves, it says in the WORD, (MATTHEW 10:16); we must know what, and who we are battling.

I have a friend who talks fluently about the energy flow of music; negative and positive; and what we listen to reinforce what we have projecting from us. Our moods, our souls, our bodies, and minds, all these are affected by the negative and positive aspects of the music we listen to. As I write these things, I am reminded that it applies to the media of all types as well; and I will get into that in a moment. First I would like to emphasize that the people in charge of these mediums are only responsible for their own actions, and beliefs; what Satan has done to influence their minds and hearts, as far as the content of said mediums is strictly on his tab.

Something of a grand scale is coming to my mind; I thank YOU for it, my LORD JESUS. I see Satan standing before the Throne of LORD JESUS, the fury of HIS anger in HIS magnificent eyes, as HE looks upon HIS defeated enemy; Satan bowing his knee to the LORDSHIP of LORD JESUS CHRIST; his tongue speaking the only truth that he is capable of speaking-that JESUS is LORD. His life is displayed and he is giving account of all he has done in the earth as well as what he did in Heaven as Lucifer. All of the lies, and deceit that he has instigated; all of the lives he has destroyed; each of them giving him a hopeless stare of hatred as they are thrown into the Lake of Fire.

I am shown things like that, and that is where my mind is; on spiritual things. I write them as I see them. Ok, back to the media, and what is brought across to each of us experiencing it. Newspapers write what they are fed by reporters; but what of the good news? Satan has us programmed to accept only bad news, and to see it as interesting. I would say that some of his comments to the individual reading is "I'm glad it's not happening to me." Then when something bad does happen to them, it's "Why me?" "What did I do wrong, GOD?" All of which are planted in the mind or played on the screen of a person's mind; especially the last one; trying to put the blame on yourself or GOD when it's actually Satan who is responsible.

I am acquainted with this tactic. If I can get you who are reading this to realize the dangers of an "open" mind, I will have succeeded in one of my goals for this book. Another goal of this book is to teach freedom from the shackles of sin, by the WORD of GOD, and my own experiences; to teach of the tactics of our enemy, and let people know they are not alone in their struggles (like I have for way too many years).

TV is just too big of a subject to tackle in a few paragraphs or even in a chapter. I could write a book on the dangers of secular TV. Allow me to say this, though, I see society being moved to a position where it will accept almost *anything*; it's been happening ever since the development of the first TV set. The spirit of what is being offered on the TV is frightening. Hero worship in sports; fornication and adultery in sitcoms, single sex relationships in families; hatred and racism to out and out *war*; all this is being portrayed and entered into the homes of millions of people. Satan just spoke to me and said," and what's my little book going to do?" As if I wouldn't catch that it wasn't of me; if it helps one person to come to freedom, I have done something. And another thing, my book will do what FATHER GOD wants to do with it, to *whom* HE wants to do it to, all to HIS glory.

Chapter 10

The story of David and Bath-Sheba is one of great importance when it comes to sin, and the results of it in our lives. We know that David killed to have Bath-Sheba for his wife. The LORD took their first child, as HE was displeased with David for the thing in which he did. After Nathan spoke the Word of the LORD, David repented. Bath-Sheba bore yet another son to David; Solomon, who ended up succeeding David as King of Israel. You know the story, you say? How about that of Job? His sin of pride had a happy ending, as did David's. The LORD GOD *is* a just GOD, yet is merciful. The Bible is filled with images of sin and the resulting judgment of GOD for that sin.

It says in the WORD:

Be not wise in thine own eyes: fear the LORD, and depart from evil.

(PROVERBS 3:7.)

I was wondering about the fear of the LORD, and LORD JESUS led me to write about it. It *is* a good thing to fear GOD, for it says in LUKE 12:5:

"But I will forewarn you whom ye shall fear: fear HIM, which after HE hath killed hath power to cast into Hell; yea, I say unto you, fear HIM. "

(LUKE 12:5.)

But the deal is this: it goes against the grain of my old nature, to *fear*; for fear is an emotion that we are taught from long ago is not good to feel. Stop dwelling in the old nature, you say? Of course, you are right; but this is a battle that rages on from the time you become a Child of GOD. Putting on the new man (EPHESIANS 4:24), and keeping him on, is my problem. Trying to fear FATHER GOD and love HIM at the same time, is difficult for me. I do love HIM, and have the problem of seeing HIM as my *FATHER*, when my own relationship with my earthly Dad wasn't that good. I didn't really know my Dad that well, and what I did know, I didn't like or respect. I guess that's the deal: I need to learn to respect the authority that my Holy Heavenly FATHER has over me; which is complete and total, including what HIS decision of my Eternal reward is; and get to know HIM personally.

There are different types of fear. There is of course, GODLY fear, and what does this mean? Do we fear HIM for the sake of what HE can do to us? What about fearing *HIM*, as in fearing to disappoint HIM, or displease HIM by doing or not doing what HE asks us to do, or not to do. Those are the ones that I am trying to manufacture for my own life's sake; I would think that I wouldn't have to produce them myself, but be given them, and I *have* been asking for them for quite some time. Maybe this is the time for HIM to give them to me.

The fear of the LORD is the beginning of knowledge.

(PROVERBS 1:7.)

What *is* the fear of the LORD? And why does it begin the path to knowledge? Does it mean the Knowledge of GOD; or the knowledge *of* GOD; of HIS existence, and the truth that HE *is*? And for the sake of semantics, what about the LORD JESUS? Is it talking about fearing HIM, for HE *is* the LORD? I believe, yes; though when King Solomon wrote the PROVERBS, LORD JESUS hadn't come to this earth yet, so HE was talking about the LORD GOD, our Holy Heavenly FATHER. I have a GODLY fear of LORD JESUS, in that I fear being caught unawares, or in the midst of doing something evil when HE returns. That keeps me on the straight and narrow path; which is something else that I pray for us.

The fear of the LORD is a beautiful thing; it is a profound reverence and awe toward GOD. Have you ever thought of fear as a beautiful thing?

The fear of the LORD *is* the instruction of wisdom.

(PROVERBS 15:33.)

I pray for wisdom and knowledge each and every morning, and from the WORD just written here, that ties in with the fear of the LORD. To me, as I have been instructed by the HOLY SPIRIT, to have wisdom *is* to walk in the fear of GOD, and my LORD JESUS.

IF any of you lack wisdom, let him ask of GOD, that giveth to all *men* liberally, and upbraideth not, and it shall be given him.

(JAMES 1:5.)

Have you ever thought about King Solomon, and the request he made of GOD?

In Gibeon the LORD appeared to Solomon in a dream by night: and GOD said, Ask what I shall give thee. And Solomon said, Thou hast shown unto Thy servant David my father great mercy, according as he walked before Thee in truth, and in righteousness, and in uprightness of heart with Thee; and Thou hast kept for him this great kindness, that Thou hast given him a son to sit on his throne as *it is* this day. And now, oh LORD my GOD, Thou hast made Thy servant king instead of David my father: and I *am but* a little child: I know not *how* to go out or to come in. And Thy servant *is* in the midst of Thy people which Thou hast chosen, a great people, that cannot be numbered nor counted for multitude. Give therefore Thy servant an understanding heart to judge Thy people, that I may discern between good and bad: for who is able to judge this Thy so great of people? And the speech pleased the LORD, that Solomon had asked this thing. And GOD said unto him, because thou hast asked this thing, and hast not asked for thyself long life; neither has asked for riches for thyself, nor asked the life of thine enemies; but hast asked for thyself understanding to discern judgment; Behold, I have done according to thy words: lo, I have given thee a wise and an understanding heart; so there was none like thee before thee, neither after thee shall any arise like unto thee. And I have also given thee that which thou hast not asked, both riches and honor: so that there shall not be any among the kings like unto thee all thy days. And if thou will walk in MY ways, to keep MY statutes and MY commandments, as thy father David did walk, then I will lengthen thy days.

(1ˢᵗ KINGS 3:5-14.)

I think that is awesome; no one like him before him, and no one like him after him. All he wanted was an understanding heart, so he could rule Israel; and the LORD GOD was *pleased* by his request, and gave him all those other things, too. Oh, that I could be as pleasing in FATHER GOD's sight as Solomon was. I am my own worst critic; maybe, just maybe, I am pleasing in GOD's eyes, just because I have the blood of HIS SON covering me, and I believe in LORD JESUS. I am receiving the wisdom and understanding, the knowledge and reverent fear of HIM on a daily basis as I ask for these things each morning, not only for myself, but for my flock, and for the entire Body of CHRIST past, present and future.

I love the story of Job, in that it was not enough for Job to simply shut his mouth, from all the words he had spoken; GOD brought him to the point of utter humility and repentance just by showing him a portion of who HE is. I love his words:

"I know that Thou can do every *thing*, and *that* no thought can be withholden from Thee. Who *is* he that hideth counsel without knowledge? Therefore have I uttered that I understood not; things too wonderful for me, which I knew not. Hear, I beseech Thee, and I will speak: I will demand of Thee, and declare Thou unto me. I have heard of Thee by the hearing of the ear: but now mine eye seeth Thee. Wherefore I abhor *myself*, and repent in dust and ashes."

(JOB 42:2-6.)

I love humility; it is a quality that I had sought of FATHER GOD to be in my mate as well. Pray with me now:

FATHER GOD, in Your Name, my Holy LORD JESUS, I come to You to praise You, three as One. Praise You for Your magnificent Mercy which You have shown in abundance upon me. Praise You for Your Grace, which *is* sufficient for me. You have known me from the foundation of the world and are fulfilling Your Holy perfect will in my life as we speak. I praise You for this. You know my heart's desire, and I ask that You would fulfill it per Your WORD. Delight ourselves in You, my Holy LORD JESUS, and You will give us the desires of our heart. I ask now that You would continue to lead me in Thy HOLY SPIRIT for everything that I do and say, think and feel, believe and ask for, all to Thy glory, in Your Name, my Holy LORD JESUS I ask these things. I love you, Amen.

Chapter 11

I was just laying in bed and FATHER GOD spoke to me (it is 2:30 in the AM), I told HIM, in my LORD JESUS' Name that I love it when HE speaks to me, for it tells me that HE loves me. It is this that HE spoke to me: HE led me in a conversation entailing the need to show my readers all about HIM (that which LORD JESUS will reveal through me in this book). HE showed me that I may be spending too much time talking about Satan, and too little time talking about HIM. HE told me that I don't want it to seem that I am glorifying our enemy in *any* way. It is my goal now to teach what I am shown to you, my readers; starting with this: FATHER GOD *loves* each and every one of us. This may seem like milk to some of you, but I believe we can never take FATHER GOD' s love for granted; that we can never talk too much about or dwell too much on HIS love for us.

HE has provided the way in which we can, and are HIS Children! Just thinking about it makes my heart warm and fuzzy; thinking about HIM sitting there on HIS Throne, beside our LORD and Savior, watching over us; they are closer than our own breath. I just looked at the clock and it says 3:16, as in JOHN 3:16. GOD leads in the most unique ways. I was shivering just now, and HE led me to get a shirt on, to warm up. Even when I don't have the sense to get out of the rain, HE will show me the correct path and lead me upon it.

Even though most all Christians know these verses, they bear repeating:

For GOD so loved the world, that HE sent HIS only begotten SON, that whosoever believeth in HIM should not perish, but have everlasting life. For GOD sent not HIS SON into the world to condemn the world; but that the world through HIM might be saved.

(JOHN 3:16,17.)

And hope maketh not ashamed; because the love of GOD is shed abroad in our hearts by the HOLY GHOST which is given unto us.

(ROMANS 5:5.)

But GOD commendeth HIS love toward us, in that, while we were yet sinners, CHRIST died for us.

(ROMANS 5:8.)

There is no more precious gift of love than that of the HOLY SPIRIT, that is, next to LORD JESUS dying for us, to set us free. It is 3 minutes till 4:00 AM, and FATHER GOD wants me to talk about HIS love. GOD waits for me to wake up, then speaks to me; this just makes my heart *glad*. I know HE is watching over my dreams; I had to pray just then, for HIS leading in the HOLY SPIRIT, for I do not doubt HIM, but rather myself; and I was led to pray for my confidence to be of my LORD JESUS, and my Holy Heavenly FATHER, and not in my ability.

To take Ones's own SON and send HIM to this earth, to be mistreated and ultimately crucified for our sakes, oh, what love is that? To know that HIS wrath is coming, and the only way out from it is to provide the purest of sacrifices to HIMSELF; the truth that HE had to turn HIS back on HIS own SON when HE had all the sins of the world on HIS shoulders, what kind of pain is that? The love in that is beyond my comprehension.

Let us talk about one of FATHER GOD's attributes that we should *all* be thankful for: HIS goodness. It is one of the fruits of the SPIRIT, and is what leads us to repentance (ROMANS 2:4). In my own life, this has been the only thing that has kept me alive, as in this body. Each and every time I would sin, FATHER GOD's Grace would cover me, and HIS goodness would lead me right back to HIS Throne to seek HIS face and HIS forgiveness (which HE has given every time. This humbles me greatly). I believe that this quality of goodness in our own lives is that of FATHER GOD's in us; HE has imparted this quality in us, and allowed us to emulate HIM. Don't you just love HIM?

I am waiting patiently for the day that I can just run up to HIM and jump in HIS lap and hug my Heavenly FATHER, who has so patiently brought me out of darkness and into the light of HIS SON, my LORD JESUS CHRIST. It is my sincere hope that every one of you reading this now will share in my expectations; for we will see it realized very soon. Isn't that exciting?! It does, however make me think about the lost, and my heart aches for those who still turn their back on the truth. My life has been one of constant leading of the HOLY SPIRIT; protected from the evils of the world, though I have dipped my bill more than once, to my deepest regret. Again, I repent, thanks to my FATHER's goodness.

> For as many as are led by the SPIRIT of GOD, they are the sons of GOD. For you have not received the spirit of bondage again to fear; but you have received the SPIRIT of adoption, whereby we cry, Abba, FATHER. The SPIRIT itself beareth witness with our spirit, that we are the Children of GOD: and if Children, then heirs; heirs of GOD, and joint heirs with CHRIST; if so be that we suffer with *HIM*, that we may also be glorified together.
>
> (ROMANS 8:14-17.)

LORD JESUS has been given *everything* since being glorified upon HIS return to HIS Heavenly Home. We shall share in that inheritance; and I speak this by HIS magnificent Grace. I am reminded of the parable of the talents by my LORD JESUS. The WORD says:

"His LORD said unto him, well done, *thou* good and faithful servant: thou hast been faithful over a few things, I will make thee ruler over many things: enter thou into the joy of thy LORD."

(MATTHEW 25:21.)

They are the words that I long to hear from my LORD; well done. It has been a long road for me; one of many mistakes and bad decisions; willful sinning, which I am thankful for, in that I can be compassionate towards those that do, and have done the same things.

It is my desire to do as the WORD instructs. One thing that I have often wondered is how to worship FATHER GOD in spirit and truth; (JOHN 4:23,24) I would guess that the place to start is the word "worship." How does one worship FATHER GOD? Scenes come to mind of me lying prostrate with my hands before me chanting, "oh, GOD, oh GOD, I worship Thee!" It sounds funny to me for a couple of reasons; in my first book, I told of a prayer time where I was allowed to feel my hands and arms as they had a special place before the Throne; I was prostrate then, too, with my hands out in front of me. I don't now, nor have I ever felt the need to chant to GOD; speak, and pray, yes. To worship HIM, to me means to "stand in awe, and sin not…" (PSALMS 4:4), meaning to honor HIM by not sinning, and be awestruck at HIS magnificence, and HIS Holiness; HIS terrible majesty (JOB 37:22)

To worship HIM in spirit does mean to me communing with HIM, speaking to HIM in the SPIRIT language of the HOLY SPIRIT; recognizing the need for humility, conveying love for him in body, mind, soul, and spirit. To worship in truth would be the epitome of obeying HIS WORD. I had thought at one time that reading aloud the WORD, and speaking words of worship was enough; but it goes way beyond that. Obedience to his authority as GOD and FATHER of us, HIS Children, to acknowledging the truth of the WORD as it applies to our daily life, is all a part of worshipping in truth (to me).

What I am about to write is really quite wonderful and it happened to *me*. It is too dear to my heart to not include it in this book. It took place about a year ago, and there are parts of the experience that the

LORD has taken away, to prevent pride from forming in me. I am content with what remains.

As a bonus and a blessing, FATHER GOD and my LORD JESUS took me by the hand and brought me to the Throne of Grace. There are obviously not the appropriate words to describe what I experienced there; but I will try.

I had my hands up, lying down on the bed, praying in the HOLY GHOST. There is so much more that happened, I cannot tell you fully if I remembered all of it. I remember the LORD pulling on my hands and arms, as if to pull me free of this body. As my resistance faded, and submission ensued, I released my spirit to the HOLY SPIRIT and was then taken by the HOLY SPIRIT to the place where all I could do, all I wanted to do was worship GOD. The man-made praise was gone; there was no place for it. There was only room for pure worship. Like it says in the WORD, the FATHER seeketh those who will worship HIM in SPIRIT and in truth. That's what I was doing, all led by my LORD JESUS through HIS HOLY SPIRIT. I felt bodily displaced; like I was lying on the bed, but was somewhere altogether in Heaven. The peace; oh, the love; I was lying on the bed, but was before the Throne of GOD.

My LORD JESUS was leading the prayers, but at some point, They allowed me to ask what I would, so I did. I asked for my children's salvation; my flock, for salvation; the finishing of the will of GOD in my life; the completion of the books They wanted me to finish, and be read by everyone who They wanted to read them. The absolute freedom to ask and receive anything according to the FATHER's will was given! HE wanted me to have all these things, and to know that HE loves us; desperately, and completely. I asked for what needed to be done for all my heart to love HIM; all. FATHER GOD knew that I had a bad coughing spell coming up, so They gently set me back down on the bed, still worshipping Them. The reality of the Throne is that there is nothing impossible to GOD; I felt it. I *knew* it with no doubts; I still do.

In discussing the event of Satanic opposition to becoming like LORD JESUS, and worshipping the FATHER of light in spirit and truth, it is necessary to take into consideration where our help comes from: to gain in strength in times of adversity, one must realize that problems we encounter are a way that FATHER GOD strengthens us; PROVERBS 10:29 says that the way of the LORD is strength to the upright. One of my friends comes to mind at this time. Almost every conceivable problem that could arise has plagued this person, all at the same time. They are wondering just what they did to deserve their present state. Strength is waning, the drive to continue is all but used up; and yet, in the midst of all this, they found the motivation to do the right thing. They responded to the evil in the way LORD JESUS wanted them to (this person is a Child of GOD).

I can do all things through CHRIST, which strengthens me.

(PHILIPPIANS 4:13.)

Including enduring the temptation to take the easy way out; pride is evil, but I am proud of my friend for seeking the GODLY way through their troubles.

Not that I speak in respect of want: for I have learned, in whatsoever state I am, *therewith* to be content. I know both how to be abased, and I know how to abound: everywhere and in all things I am instructed both to be full and to be hungry, both to abound and to suffer need.

(PHILIPPIANS 4:11,12.)

Have you ever heard of putting GOD in a box? One time at my church the HOLY SPIRIT spoke, and the first thing that came out of the mouth of the person doing the interpretation of the tongues, was "Don't put me in a box." This was LORD JESUS speaking; I think I was one of the only ones to hear this part; but it stuck with me. The WORD says:

Giving thanks unto the FATHER, which hath made us meet to be partakers of the inheritance of the saints in light: who hath delivered us from the power of darkness, and hath translated *us* into the Kingdom of HIS dear SON: in whom we have redemption through

HIS blood, *even* the forgiveness of sins: Who is the image of the invisible GOD, the first born of every creature: For by HIM were all things created, that are in Heaven, and that are in earth, visible and invisible, whether *they be* thrones, or dominions, or principalities, or powers: all things were created by HIM, and for HIM: and HE is before all things, and by HIM all things consist. And HE is the head of the Body, the Church; Who is the beginning, the first born from the dead; that in all *things* HE might have the preeminence. For it pleased *the FATHER* that in HIM should all fullness dwell; and, having made peace through the blood of HIS cross, by HIM to reconcile all things unto HIMSELF; by HIM, I *say*, whether *they be* things in earth, or things in Heaven.

(COLOSSIANS 1:12-20.)

Whew!

"I am Alpha and Omega, the beginning and the ending," saith the LORD, which is, and which was, and which is to come, the Almighty.

(REVELATION 1:8.)

As John witnessed,

And I turned to see the voice that spake with me. And being turned, I saw seven golden candlesticks; and in the midst of the seven candlesticks *one* like unto the SON of man, clothed with a garment down to the foot, and girt about the paps with a golden girdle. HIS head and *HIS* hairs *were* white like wool, as white as snow; and HIS eyes *were* as a flame of fire; and HIS feet like unto fine brass, as if they burned in a furnace; and HIS voice like the sound of many waters. And HE had in HIS hand seven stars: and out of HIS mouth went a sharp two-edged sword: and HIS countenance *was* as the sun shineth in HIS strength. And when I saw HIM, I fell at HIS feet as dead. And HE laid HIS right hand upon me, saying unto me, "Fear not; I am the first and the last: I *am* HE that liveth, and was dead; and, behold, I am alive forever more, Amen; and have the keys of Hell and of death."

(REVELATION 1:12-18.)

LORD JESUS CHRIST is *glorified* now. You couldn't put HIM in a box if you had to; but there are still people who try, deceiving themselves into thinking HE doesn't even matter! If you know of someone who thinks like this, show them the scriptures in this book; plant the seeds of righteousness in their hearts. The WORD is alive; it won't come back void.

This next verse is one that thrills me, for it lets me know that GOD's face and eyes are everywhere:

And I saw a great white Throne, and HIM that sat on it, from whose face the earth and the heaven fled away, and there was found no place for them.

(REVELATION 20:11.)

We're going to see that Throne someday *soon*. There is another verse telling of LORD JESUS' omnipotence, and omnipresence even while HE was on this earth:

"Your father Abraham rejoiced to see MY day: and he saw *it* and was glad." Then said the Jews unto HIM, Thou art not yet fifty years old, and hast Thou seen Abraham? JESUS said unto them," Verily, verily, I say unto you, before Abraham was, I AM."

(JOHN 8:56-58.)

I know that you who are reading this now probably know all these things; and have read them many times. But did you ever stop to consider that each and every time you read the WORD it can have pertinence to situations presently in your life? Base knowledge like what LORD JESUS and FATHER GOD are right *now* can have immediate and lasting effect on your lives; especially in your prayer life. I see LORD JESUS as I have been shown HIM by HIMSELF in my face. I still at times, when I will look at myself in the mirror see the outline of HIS beautiful face in my features. I acknowledge HIM as I look on; HE will sometimes smile at me through my own face, and I see the love in my eyes, coming directly from HIM. I am definitely blessed.

Chapter 12

Do you sometimes wish that you could be more in and to the Kingdom of GOD? What do you suppose is holding you back from it; the sin of judging people? Like I did just now; the HOLY SPIRIT caught me thinking judgmental thoughts about a brother of ours. The original thought probably came from Satan in my mind, then I took it the rest of the way towards judging my brother.

> Therefore, you are inexcusable, oh man, whoever you are who judge, for in whatever you judge another you condemn yourself; for you who judge practice the same things.

> (ROMANS 2:1.)

My brother in CHRIST feels that all LORD JESUS does is ask questions; i.e., putting HIM in a box. As I reflected upon the thought of him doing this, I started to laugh out loud, at thinking that is all HE does, when LORD JESUS has *all* of creation in HIS control. I judged my brother unworthily, for now that I am convicted of it, I am guilty of doing the same. It is the WORD; and LORD JESUS goes on to say:

> "Judge not, that you be not judged. For with what judgment you judge, you will be judged; and with the measure you use, it will be measured back to you."

> (MATTHEW 7:1,2.)

If I can get a hold of this point, I will be very happy; for I have had this happen to me on several occasions. My LORD JESUS shows me through HIS HOLY SPIRIT that I am judging; HE shows me what I am doing that mirrors what the person I was judging is doing. In this case, I was putting LORD JESUS in a box. When I pray, I tend to think of LORD JESUS as inside my heart, and not on the Throne in Heaven above. Then at times I am praying, and don't consider HIS glorification and authority over me and the entirety of creation. And for that, I beg YOUR forgiveness, my Holy LORD JESUS.

It is so easy to do; all Satan has to do is plant a thought about something someone has said that caught me wrong, or at the wrong time, and…off I go, judging my brothers and sisters. Do you see the immediate righteous judgments of FATHER GOD? For as many times in a day that we judge people, HE is right there witnessing each and every one of them, acting upon them according to HIS WORD. "With the measure you use, it will be measured back to you," this is not done on Judgment Day only; it is done on a daily basis. FATHER GOD, LORD JESUS, and Their HOLYSPIRIT are present with us. And if I may, it applies to *all* people; Children of GOD, and those who are not yet in the Kingdom.

At one time, I was told not to judge a person by what they do, but by what they have. That is all the voice would tell me; and I asked what the last part of that statement meant, to no avail. That's when I considered it a voice of schizophrenia. It may have been Satan trying to deceive me into judging, period. But let me think this one through… don't judge what a person docs? That part makes sense; but by what a person has? Did the voice mean who they had in their heart? Meaning the LORD JESUS, or if they were still children of the Devil? That at least would make sense, and if that was the HOLY SPIRIT that told me that, I beg forgiveness, I did not know. That is the way I will take that comment to me; that I will judge by who the person has in their heart, and accept them as such; brothers and sisters in my LORD JESUS, or fellow human beings.

One of my brothers in CHRIST at the church I go to felt my judgment one time; I was, at the time looking at his attire, and his hygiene, and judging him as unworthy. Sick of me, wasn't it? That is totally against the WORD, and I admit to this wrong faithfully in front of my Heavenly FATHER. And, according to LORD JESUS' words, he gave back to me just as I gave to him. So LORD JESUS orchestrated the return feeling my brother gave me, through giving me a look of his own, that I wasn't part of the Body of CHRIST, or his brother. It worked out in the end, though; after seeing me talking to, and praying with a brother and fellow acquaintance, he came over and introduced himself, and we shook hands. I saw him in a very different light that day, thanks to the HOLY SPIRIT (and a lot of HOLY GHOST humility). I would rather be humbled with the humble, than have pride with the proud.

Consider this: if we are guilty of doing the same things when we judge, then those who judge us as hypocrites are guilty of hypocrisy as well; right? But we can't say, "See, you do it, too." For this doesn't do anything but end the conversation right there, or cause a bitter argument over who is right. Our words are to be from Heavenly things, and about Heavenly things. It should be our goal to overcome any obstacles in our way that keep us from ministering to and witnessing to our lost brothers and sisters; also to perfect the saints, and work in the "fields" of this world; keeping ourselves unspotted from the world.

What does it mean to keep oneself "unspotted" from the world? Dalmatians come to mind; I'm sorry, Satan just put that in my mind to get me thinking in a humorous way. It isn't a funny subject, if one thinks about it. FATHER GOD is serious; it comes from JAMES 1:27. We are tethered to this world, but we are not *of* this world; meaning that we still have to operate by the laws of this world, but our Home is in Heaven with our LORD JESUS. It even says in the WORD:

> But GOD, who is rich in mercy, for HIS great love wherewith HE loved us, even when we were dead in sins, hath quickened us together with CHRIST, (by grace you are saved). And has raised *us* up together, and made *us* sit together in Heavenly *places* in CHRIST JESUS: that in the ages to come HE might show the exceeding riches of HIS grace in *HIS* kindness toward us through CHRIST JESUS.
>
> (EPHESIANS 2:4-7.)

As it stands right now, I only *wish* that I understood what it means to "sit together in Heavenly places in CHRIST JESUS." It makes it sound like we are *supposed* to be in Heaven with LORD JESUS, even as we are on this earth. Somehow that makes sense to me; let me tell you another true story of a time I was out with one of my friends at a place I called Prettyview; it was a beautiful place with a live stream running through it, and lots of wooded areas to explore. It is where I received many of the revelations I have written in these books of mine. It is also where Satan did a lot of stealing of the things the HOLY SPIRIT wanted me to explore in HIM. I didn't at the time understand what was happening, and as the things were stolen, I just retained the memory that I *had* something important that I no longer had. A lot of regrets came to me at that time also, because of this.

Let us get back to the story of how living in the presence of the LORD is like sitting with HIM in Heavenly places. My friend and I were just sitting on the hood of my car talking religion, when all of the sudden I felt the leading to include him in a prayer to LORD JESUS. I stood up, and looking directly at the light of the moon, started talking to the LORD; all with my friend right there beside me. I spoke of my friend in the present tense, and prayed repentance for the both of us, as we had been drinking wine coolers, and were acting kind of rebellious at the time. My friend didn't like what I was doing at first, but as the SPIRIT came over us, he too felt the need to repent. We dumped out the remaining coolers, and headed back home. All was well after that, and my friend had a taste of being in the presence of the LORD, even while sinning. That was probably 20 or so years ago, and I still remember it like it was yesterday. My friend remembers it, too.

Remember the widows and the fatherless? Keeping oneself unspotted from the world; this is what FATHER GOD's WORD tells us to do. Again, how does one remain "unspotted," especially in the world of this day and age; where most people are involved in any one of thousands of religious sects, and religions from Christianity to the Eastern religions, to cults and even Satan worshipping. Wars and rumors of wars; that's how LORD JESUS described the beginning of the end; make sure no one deceives you, HE said. We have talked at length about the deception of Satan in our lives; now I want to ask you a question, and it has bothered me for some time now. What exactly is the "world?" For GOD so loved the "world" it says. This would obviously mean the people of the world; but this seemingly contradictive phraseology would suggest that there is a part of this earth that is worldly apart from the people of this earth. The world of sin is a large part of this "world," and to be avoided at all costs.

I believe what I am attempting to reach is the "spirit" of this world. The deceitfulness of riches; the cares of this world that choke out the WORD, and make us unfruitful (MATTHEW 13:22); I might list a few from my own life: like the need of new furniture; the prestige of a newer car, that gets good gas mileage; making sure that my children have their college educations in order; all these things are of the world, when the truth of the matter is, in each case, pride is the motivation; and pride is of this world. My children need to know the truth, that making money is not the prime goal of life. Doing the will of FATHER GOD is the most important thing to accomplish in this world (MATTHEW 12:50) to be the brother and sister of the LORD JESUS.

One thing I do to try to keep myself unspotted from the world is to not let money run my life. Since I am dead, and my life is hid with CHRIST in GOD, I consider that I have no possessions, for all that I have *is* the LORD JESUS' property. I am simply using it. This includes any money I receive for work done to HIS glory. It takes a conscious effort to think this way; to consider that any money in the bank is HIS; that the car I drive is LORD JESUS', and ultimately this life *is* HIS, to do with as it pleases HIM. I want to please HIM; as I know you reading this do as well.

As I was lying on the couch, looking up towards the Throne, I asked LORD JESUS a question. I asked HIM if HE ever got tired of me; tired of the way I am; and in the same sentence, I rephrased it; no, rather the way I chose to be. Because of my sins of pride and complacency, and an occasional bout with adulterous looks and judging people, I thought about it for a moment, and then voiced the response, I now choose to be holy. LORD JESUS showed me, and then told me that only FATHER, SON, and HOLY GHOST *are* HOLY. I can choose *to* be, but only They *ARE* Holy. They are the only ones that are *I AM*. Remember what FATHER GOD told Moses by the burning bush? "Tell them *I AM* hath sent you." My LORD JESUS, in showing me this, made it clear that HE is still teaching me, and by teaching me, I can teach you, as well. That in itself tells me that HE isn't tired of me. Praise HIM!

As I was going through my previously written papers, I came upon an insight that is really appropriate. It is about happiness. The LORD gives me these insights at various times, to be used at a future time. It most certainly uses the WORD as HIS inspiration; I will use HIS leading in the HOLY SPIRIT to take it to the next level. It goes like this: Happiness. It is coveted, sought after by most human beings. Do you know what the Bible says will bring happiness to you? The man who finds wisdom, and gets understanding is happy (PROVERBS 3:13); happy is everyone that retains her (wisdom and understanding) (PROVERBS 3:18); he that has mercy on the poor, happy is he (PROVERBS 14:21); whoso trusts in the LORD, happy is he (PROVERBS 16:20). Happy is the man who fears always: but he that hardens his heart shall fall into mischief (PROVERBS 28:14). Where there is no vision, the people perish: but he that keeps the law, happy is he (PROVERBS 29:18). Happy is he that condemns not himself in the thing which he allows. (ROMANS 14:22) If you suffer for righteousness' sake, happy are you (1ˢᵗ PETER 3:14); if you be reproached for the Name of CHRIST, happy are you (1ˢᵗ PETER 4:14). And, Behold, we count them happy which endure (JAMES 5:11).

As long as we are talking about happiness, I want to tell you what makes me happy. Blessing my LORD and FATHER, finding obedience in my character, and obeying their commandments; this makes me happy. When I know I have done the best I can to please them, and succeeded, this makes me happy. Deep depression comes over me when I sin. I believe this is true of all of the Body of CHRIST; it is called remorse, and it leads in its true form, to repentance by the goodness of FATHER GOD.

The reason I confess my sins so readily after committing them is because I can no longer operate in the state of depression. That, and the truth that I can't live life knowing I have unconfessed sin in my life. I wouldn't and won't be caught dead with unconfessed sin; at least those that I have committed intentionally. I believe that FATHER GOD's grace covers the ones that we are not aware of. Anyway, the HOLY

SPIRIT lets me know of any sins that I have committed unknowingly, and leads me to the FATHER in my LORD JESUS' Name to be forgiven.

Back when I drank I got used to living in a depressed state. Now that I don't drink hard liquor anymore (I only drink a little bit of red wine now and then), I cannot stand to be in a depressed frame of mind. I do take anti-depressants for the feelings that accompany the schizophrenia. All in all, I am a pretty stable guy, what with all the medications I take, and my priceless relationship with my LORD JESUS, and the FATHER of Light. The combination of the two, joined by the HOLY SPIRIT of GOD, leads me to confess my sins before FATHER GOD in humility and repentance. Aside from the time HE judged me, and the three of them left my heart, (I am not fully convinced this wasn't a hallucination of voice and vision), HE has never turned HIS back on me, and I perceive HE never will. It is HIS WORD (I will never leave thee, nor forsake thee- HEBREWS 13:5).

What I experienced was likely an elaborate hallucination; but you be the judge. Read my first book. As I perceived it, FATHER GOD judged me for continually sinning in wicked imaginations (which thing HE hates). FATHER, SON and HOLY SPIRIT left my heart for what seemed like an eternity, but was actually only a few moments. After HE gave me time to think about what I had done, FATHER GOD led me to ask LORD JESUS back into my heart. It's a great story, and what's more, it's true.

I was lying in bed after writing on this book, when satanic thoughts of lustful situations came into my mind, causing my loins to react. I commanded Satan twice in my LORD JESUS' Name; the first time, I commanded him to back away and take his images with him. He left for approximately 30 seconds. When he came at me the second time, I felt the leading to command him to leave, taking his seeds and the effect of those seeds with him, and not come back till the morning (when I will deal with him at that time).

At what point of Satan's attacks do you just give up and let the images dance in your head, giving him free roam to come and go as he pleases? If you only command Satan in LORD JESUS' Name to leave, he *will* come back again, guaranteed. If you command him with all of his seeds and the effect of those seeds to leave and not come back for a specified period of time, he must obey if it is done in LORD JESUS' Name. The WORD says:

> Submit yourselves to GOD. Resist the Devil, and he will flee from you.
>
> (JAMES 4:7.)

It *is* just that simple. However, recognizing satanic thoughts is a matter of deduction. Thoughts come from one of three sources: GOD, Satan, or ourselves. If you are not generating them, they are either GOD's input through HIS SPIRIT, or they are of Satan. Consider who it glorifies; LORD JESUS and the FATHER, or self, and its five senses. I knew the ones I just experienced were of Satan, because they had "lust" written all over them. I believe that LORD JESUS allowed Satan to come at me those two times so I could write about the experience, and let you reading this know as well.

I have been shown a great sin preventative. Besides the knowledge of the truth that FATHER GOD judges sin, there is a little thought of truth that *should* blow you away, and start you thinking seriously.

It is the WORD of GOD; and it goes like this:

> "...For there is nothing covered, that shall not be revealed; and hid, that shall not be known."
>
> (MATTHEW 10:26)

And I saw the dead, small and great, stand before GOD; and the books were opened: and another book was opened, which is *the book* of life: and the dead were judged out of those things which were written in the books, according to their works.

> (REVELATION 20:12)

Have you ever had the feeling that you were being watched? Aside from me being schizophrenic, there is a feeling present that I believe comes directly from the Throne to me. That is the knowledge that every person who has ever been alive is watching what I am doing right at this very moment. Because I believe that everything we do is written down in the "books," right down to every thought, every motive, and every decision we make and do. We will all stand and give account for every idle word we speak (MATTHEW 12:36); and because we are in effect *in* Eternity, that is to say that all of time is a speck *in* Eternity, and FATHER GOD is everywhere and every when, omnipresent, HE is actually there; LORD JESUS *is* there playing out what they already know is going to happen. Some call this predestination. I just consider it, and stand in awe of FATHER, SON, and HOLY SPIRIT, and love them with all my heart, soul, mind and strength.

Even when I am intentionally sinning, I consider that everyone that has ever been alive is watching what I am doing; for at some point in Eternity, we will all be shown everything that has happened in this world, as we stand before GOD. The point was just given me that all that has been forgiven, by confession of our sins, is forgotten.

As far as the east is from the west, *so* far hath HE removed our transgressions from us.

(PSALMS 103:12)

Consider this: Everything that has been forgiven will not be repeated. I can receive this, for I believe FATHER GOD has forgotten these things before HIM. In REVELATION 4:6 it talks about the sea of glass like unto crystal before the Throne; I've heard it described as the sea of forgetfulness. I won't know if that is true till I get there. All of the things that are hid, and covered, as of right now, *will* be revealed; the rest is forgotten. No one really knows, do they? All we have is the WORD, and all the various versions of it dilute and change the meanings of what was originally written. I trust the King James Version. I still believe that all our works will be judged; it's just that there will be no judgment on the things that have been forgiven. REVELATION 20:12 could mean only the lost, for it speaks of the "dead" being judged by the opening of the "books." But then again, if the Book of Life is opened at that place of Judgment, could it mean that some of the "dead" are saved and written in the Lambs Book of Life? Again, no one really knows. I believe as the WORD says that the Righteous will be on HIS right hand, and the lost on HIS left. It stands to reason that those that have been in Hell will be transported to the place of the Judgment Seat of CHRIST, along with all those that have accepted CHRIST into their hearts, and are saved from the Second Death. The Judgment of all people will happen from there.

> For we must all appear before the Judgment Seat of CHRIST; that everyone may receive the things *done* in *his* body, according to that he hath done, whether *it* be good or bad.

> (2ⁿᵈ CORINTHIANS 5:10)

> And whosoever was not found written in the Book of Life was cast into the Lake of Fire.

> (REVELATION 20:15)

The Second Death is what is to be avoided at *all* costs. What we do now, in *this* day, is what will either stand or fall in the Day of Judgment. This is another reason that Satan wants us to fall to temptation; the WORD says that the wages of sin is death (ROMANS 6:23); and he wants as many as he can make fall to temptation share in his Eternal punishment. He makes his temptations look as pleasing to the senses as he can, but the end is still the same-the Lake of Fire. That is why I am writing this book; to warn you of Satan's devises, and hopefully, prayerfully set you free from his bondage to sin. LORD JESUS has made the path to Heaven an open superhighway. We who believe in HIM have Eternal Life. Sins committed by we who believe are brought before the Throne of Grace to be forgiven. Once they are forgiven, they are forgotten; forever.

Back to the innumerable people before the Throne, and the thought that they are watching me at this very moment; I know this is not true, for the Judgment hasn't happened yet. I just consider all the people, to help prevent the intentional sinning. I believe it is a gift from my LORD JESUS, and I thank HIM for it. Wouldn't it seem to add stress to my life, thinking that every one that has ever been alive is watching me? I believe I am forgiven, both now and in the Day of Judgment. I walk in repentance, and trust in my LORD JESUS with all my heart. The LORD has mercy upon me, not letting this knowledge overwhelm me. Truth to tell it isn't all the time; just in pertinent times that prevents me from sinning.

You'd be surprised at how your attitude changes, and your actions are modified when it comes to your mind that FATHER GOD and the LORD JESUS and every one standing before the Throne is aware of what you are thinking. It's a little hard to comprehend, actually. It's more by faith that I accept it. But one thing is for sure-I am sinning less and less because of it. How would you feel if you knew that the person you were judging because of the way they are dressed was aware of your thoughts? That the person you are looking and thinking lustfully at is aware of what you are thinking about them? It helps to think of it right now, for me. Some people have told me that I could tell what they were thinking before they said anything. I do not think this is a symptom of schizophrenia; I believe it is a SPIRIT led thing. I have in times past taken advantage of this; and tried to use it for my own purposes. FATHER GOD would then show me the effect of what I was planning, and disarm it. I now know HE has always had my best in mind, praise HIM!

Chapter 13

Per the HOLY SPIRIT's leading, I have been given the opportunity to make you think, and to consider; The WORD says:

This know also, that in the last days perilous times shall come. For men shall be lovers of their own selves, covetous, boasters, proud, blasphemers, disobedient to parents, unthankful, unholy, without natural affection, trucebreakers, false accusers, incontinent, fierce, despisers of those that are good, traitors, heady, high-minded, lovers of pleasures more than lovers of GOD; having a form of godliness, but denying the power thereof: from such turn away.

(2nd TIMOTHY 3:5.)

We have talked a lot about sin, and Satan; I was given the green light to talk about someone who is worthy of all praise and love, that is my LORD JESUS. Without HIM, it would not be possible to resist sin, nor would there be any reason to; all would be going to Hell, then the Lake of Fire.

Starting with HIS conception by the HOLY SPIRIT, HIS virgin birth, and the truth that HE is all man, and all GOD; HE was *the* perfect man-sinless, though HE was tempted in all ways like we are, yet without sin (HEBREWS 4:15). Let us talk about that. Through the 33 years of HIS life on this earth (I believe HE was 33 when HE was crucified), LORD JESUS endured all the temptations that we encounter here in this time; from the temptation to walk in pride, the temptation to commit adultery, the temptation to take HIS FATHER's Name in vain (HE must have hit HIS thumb with the mallet); Satan was right there to offer the worldly response. I know what LORD JESUS did though; HE denied HIMSELF, and thanked HIS FATHER for the temptations, and the leading of the HOLY SPIRIT *to* deny HIMSELF. When the pretty young girl (or guy for that matter) hit on HIM, HE denied HIMSELF, and remained pure. HE told them the truth that the WORD of GOD says, thou shalt not commit adultery; or some likened thing to that.

It is interesting to think about LORD JESUS' life before HE entered into the Ministry; before HE did the first miracle of turning the water into wine. The fact that there is no record in the Bible of HIS life except for the bout in the temple, and HIS saying that HE must be about HIS FATHER's business, and returned with Joseph and HIS mother, submitting to them, and carrying on the trade of carpenter, makes it even more interesting.

Satan must not have started his temptations just when LORD JESUS was led into the wilderness, because there were only three incidents recorded of temptation from the Devil; and if LORD JESUS was tempted like we are, Satan must have been tempting HIM all along. Did LORD JESUS command him away from HIM when HE was young? All three of the recorded temptations were of ones that would be to the SON of GOD; not we as humans. They were targeted at HIS LORDSHIP. Like the first one, Command these stones be made bread; Are you the SON of GOD or aren't you? We know what LORD JESUS said: "It is written, man shall not live by bread alone, but by every word that proceeds out of the mouth of GOD." LORD JESUS used HIMSELF, the WORD, to make Satan back down each time HE was tempted. The second temptation Satan used the WORD to try and deceive LORD JESUS; again trying to force HIS hand and show that HE was the SON of GOD. Cast thyself down, for it is written; and LORD JESUS told him again, using the WORD, "Thou shalt not tempt the LORD thy GOD." Satan used all his cards on the last temptation. All these things will I give you if you will but fall down and worship me. It's like he was saying to JESUS, if you are the SON of GOD, it would ruin your career if you would do this one thing; but I *will* give you all the kingdoms of this world for your temporary pleasure. I am so glad that LORD JESUS said what HE did next- "Get thee hence, Satan: for it is written, Thou shalt worship the LORD thy GOD, and HIM only shalt thou serve." Like it says in the WORD:

> And there are also many other things which JESUS did, the which, if they should be written every one, I suppose that even the world itself could not contain the books that should be written, Amen.
>
> (JOHN 21:25.)

I like to play with the idea that LORD JESUS was very personable, and that HE laughed a lot; consider this: visiting the earth HE was there when it was created; interacting with people that were created by HIM, and for HIM; HE had all the emotions that are common to man, so HE was able to laugh, and cry; HE was able to love, and receive love. HIS mother had to change HIS diapers when HE was little, and comfort HIM when HE was teething; all the things that we have to deal with, HE dealt with, too. I find that amazing to think about.

We have to believe in faith that HE was sinless, and I have no problem with doing that. I believe with all my being that HE went through all we do, yet without sin. HE would have had to, to be the perfect sacrifice for our sins.

Puberty must have been a hoot for HIM. I can just see HIS voice cracking as it changed. And what about being knowledgeable that HE was the SON of GOD, and learning the humility of being human? Sometimes I get the feeling that I am learning to accept being human; with all its frailties and pitfalls. LORD JESUS learned those things as well.

> Let this mind be in you, which was also in CHRIST JESUS: Who, being in the form of GOD, thought it not robbery to be equal with GOD: but made HIMSELF of no reputation, and took upon HIM the form of a servant, and was made in the likeness of men: and

being found in fashion as a man, HE humbled HIMSELF, and became obedient unto death, even the death of the cross.

(PHILIPPIANS 2:5-8.)

What are we tempted with? Are we the Children of GOD? Satan asks; tempting us to forsake the high calling we are called with. And this brings up another point that I have wondered about. The WORD says that Satan is a liar. Was he telling LORD JESUS the truth when he said this to HIM?

All this power will I give thee, and the glory of them: for that is delivered unto me; and to whomsoever I will I give it. If thou therefore wilt worship me, all shall be thine.

(LUKE 4:6,7.)

He was lying to LORD JESUS, wasn't he? He was trying to wreck LORD JESUS' future by offering HIM the temporary. It is the same with us. Satan uses the world he has been given to tempt us into taking the pleasures of sin for a season, instead of looking at the Eternal consequences of sin; the Lake of Fire. So many of the people that have set their affections on this world, and put their trust in money and power must have been given these things by Satan, through being deceived by him; or else they have been led astray by people who have been deceived by Satan.

LORD JESUS wasn't deceived by Satan; couldn't be deceived by him, for the HOLY SPIRIT was given HIM, without measure (JOHN 3:34). It is another reason that we need to continually ask for the filling of the HOLY SPIRIT on a daily basis. Our power to resist the Devil's temptations does not come from us; it comes from the HOLY SPIRIT within us; just as HE did for LORD JESUS.

FATHER GOD did some work on Satan, though; blinding his eyes from seeing LORD JESUS' true path, and darkening his understanding to the point that he thought it was the perfect thing to do to end LORD JESUS' reign on this earth by deceiving the Scribes and Chief Priests and the Pharisees into condemning HIM to death. Had Satan known what LORD JESUS' death would do, he would have done everything in his power to prevent it. Thank FATHER GOD he didn't.

LORD JESUS, when HE did finally die, went to Hell, and took the keys of Hell and of death from Satan (EPHESIANS 4:9, and REVELATION 1:18). 3 days later- HALLELUJAH!! The LORD lives!! And HE is alive forevermore (REVELATIONS 1:18).

Now LORD JESUS is back in HIS Home; sitting at the right hand of GOD HIS FATHER on the Throne of Heaven. HE has been given all things (MATTHEW 11:27) and is KING over all creation. HIS return will usher in ETERNITY for all who have trusted in HIM, giving us eternal life. LORD JESUS has *done all this for us*. HIS love for us truly does pass all knowledge; Glory to HIM!! And it was the FATHER's plan that instigated the fall of Satan, and the glorifying of HIS SON for all Eternity; PRAISE HIM!!

When I am finally Home, be it today, or years from now, I will finally be rid of this body of death, and will be able to worship FATHER GOD and LORD JESUS as I have only imagined in this life. All manmade praise and worship will be a thing of the past. I will sing praises to my LORD and FATHER with my fellow servants, the angels eternally. I will talk with the four and twenty elders that have been before the Throne. I will sing, Holy, Holy, Holy with the four beasts before the Throne. I will finally know what the 7 thunders uttered that LORD JESUS ordered sealed. I will finally be Home.

If you do not know LORD JESUS as your Savior, please accept HIM now. HE is waiting, knocking at the door of your heart at this very moment. HE *loves you*. Join me in singing praises to HIM for all Eternity by asking LORD JESUS into your heart. Believe in HIM and trust in HIM. FATHER GOD and their HOLY SPIRIT will come into your heart also. Eternal life, it is the gift of GOD; and it is yours for the asking.

The End